DESI DREAMS

~~

INDIAN IMMIGRANT WOMEN BUILD LIVES ACROSS TWO WORLDS

DESI DREAMS

*Indian Immigrant Women
Build Lives Across Two Worlds*

ASHIDHARA DAS

PRIMUS BOOKS
An imprint of Ratna Sagar P. Ltd.
Virat Bhavan
Mukherjee Nagar Commercial Complex
Delhi 110 009

Offices at
CHENNAI   KOLKATA   LUCKNOW
AGRA   AHMEDABAD   BANGALORE   COIMBATORE   DEHRADUN   GUWAHATI
HYDERABAD   JAIPUR   KANPUR   KOCHI   MADURAI   MUMBAI   PATNA   RANCHI

© *Ashidhara Das 2012*

All rights reserved. No part of this publication may be reproduced or transmitted, in any form or by any means, without permission. Any person who does any unauthorized act in relation to this publication may be liable to criminal prosecution and civil claims for damages.

First published 2012

ISBN: 978-93-80607-47-4

Published by Primus Books

Laser typeset by Digigrafics
Gulmohar Park, New Delhi 110 049

Printed at Shree Maitrey Printech Pvt Ltd, Noida

This book is meant for educational and learning purposes. The author(s) of the book has/have taken all reasonable care to ensure that the contents of the book do not violate any existing copyright or other intellectual property rights of any person in any manner whatsoever. In the event the author(s) has/have been unable to track any source and if any copyright has been inadvertently infringed, please notify the publisher in writing for corrective action.

To
my loving parents
and parents-in-law
for their inspiring example
and constant encouragement

Contents

List of Tables	ix
Preface	xi
Acknowledgements	xvii
I. At Home and at Work in the Diaspora: Theoretical Approaches and a Statistical Overview	1
II. In Search of Success in the American Workplace	32
III. Professional Women at Home and in the Immigrant Community	58
IV. The Construction of the Self	94
V. Conclusion	136
Glossary	149
Bibliography	151
Index	159

Tables

TABLE 1.1	Race and Ethnicity in the US	22
TABLE 1.2	Total Number of Asian Indians in the US	23
TABLE 1.3	Racial and Ethnic Diversity in the San Francisco Bay Area	24
TABLE 1.4	A Cross-Section of the Asian Indian Community among 8 Counties of the San Francisco-Oakland Bay Area	25
TABLE 1.5	Education Level of Asian Indians in 8 Counties of the San Francisco-Oakland Bay Area	25
TABLE 1.6	Race Divisions in the State of California	27
TABLE 1.7	Change in California's Racial Composition in the Last Decade	27

Preface

IN GENERAL, MY research has been guided by the principle that the study of cultural theories accompanied by the collection and analysis of ethnographic data is the principal foundation of the formulation of new theories of lasting value. I do not claim to have penetrated the innermost workings of the psyche of my informants, nor do I claim to have found out the ultimate truth about their lives but rather, I embarked on a journey of self-exploration with them. Many of my interviewees said that they really enjoyed talking to me as they got to talk about themselves and the issues they faced in their lives. Each encounter was different in tone for while some women were eager to air their concerns, worries, and anxieties about their lives, others wanted to present their lives as complete, fulfilled, and balanced in every way. I suppose each was speaking her own truth and she was conveying something to me even in her exaggerations, or in her evasions and silences. I am grateful to the women I interviewed for laying out their lives in front of me for me to examine and in the following chapters I will attempt to summarize some of my findings from these interviews.

As a member of the immigrant community, I know my work will be read by some members of this community, and while I was writing up the data I had collected, I was aware that some Indian Americans will regard my work as somewhat objectionable. I do not want to strengthen existing stereotypes, yet I must represent my findings impartially. On some occasions it has been hard to create a distance between myself and my subjects, especially as we are so similar, and so this has been one of the ongoing challenges of my research. I suppose all researchers identify with 'their people' at some point, and must make a conscious effort to separate their own identities from that of their subjects to create a study as objective as possible.

I was fortunate to be in an extremely inclusive university. Eminent experts in their respective fields, the professors who took me under their wing were extremely down to earth, and they went out of their way to explain new theoretical concepts to me and help me to adjust to the new academic environment. My colleagues were exceedingly friendly, including me in numerous formal as well as informal discussions both inside and outside class. Besides being exceptionally academically gifted and receptive to learning, the undergraduate students I taught in discussion sections in the course of my work as a teaching assistant in the university were invariably cordial and cooperative. However, whilst conducting some of my research, I found that my university colleagues and students sometimes raised issues that were hard to explain as they do not have the same cultural conditioning as I do. Once, I was asked about patriarchal tyranny in Asian America; after all, had not all feminists, both White and Brown, always insisted that Asian women were terribly oppressed and domestic abuse was rampant in the Indian community? I found it difficult to counter this perception, but it is not entirely correct. Yes, I had found that patriarchal authority was seldom directly questioned among Asian Indians in the US, but I had also discovered many instances where it was indirectly subverted. Equally, many Indian American women I had spoken to indicated that their priority was to hold the immigrant family together in the face of cultural marginalization by the dominant society, and they accomplished this by bolstering the self-perception of their men rather than attempting to change age-old gender habits for the sake of female rights. I was also asked: Do Indian diasporic parents not deprive their children of the opportunity to adopt normative 'American' behaviour patterns? Do they not force outdated restrictive ethnic cultural strictures on Indian American youth? I found it difficult to explain the emotional over-reliance on biological links, especially on offspring, that I had found among first generation Indian immigrants. Also, the parental response to the charge of being ethnically inferior was to assert their own ethnic moral superiority and thus, to attempt to invert normative exclusion by the mainstream population. This does not justify overbearing parental conduct, but it does explain it to some extent.

Besides being a social-theorist, I am also a parent of two children who are growing up in the US, and I am confident that my children will be able to negotiate the socio-political and cultural constraints they encounter in their daily lives with confidence in their own familial and ethnic roots as well as familiarity with American values and norms. I stand on both sides of the ethnographic researcher-subject fence, and my job as translator is sometimes hard to perform since I am invested in both sides.

Pierrette Hondagneu-Sotelo observes that gender and immigration scholarship must research how gender permeates a variety of day-to-day practices and political and economic institutional structures (1999). Rather than focusing only on women's experiences, women's empowerment, and everyday female relationships, we must study how gender is a crucial ingredient of immigration. Gender permeates and organizes a variety of practices, institutions, and identities that are incorporated in immigration. In my own research, I have studied how gender is a crucial element in the composition of the labour force, transnationalism, moral conceptualizations, and ethnic identity. It is not possible to do justice to the full range of female experiences without also studying male experiences, hence my research is as much about Indian immigrant men as it is about Indian immigrant women in the Bay Area. Hence, this work records Indian immigrant male experience alongside corresponding female experience in the US, and in this way, it belongs to the genre of gender studies more than it belongs to the genre of women's studies.

Let us now reverse the gaze and observe the observer, namely, myself. My topic of research touches close to my own life. I am not exempt from the prejudices, shortsightedness, and aspirations for upward mobility that I have described among my Indian immigrant interview subjects. I suppose that like other Indians who reside in the US, I too have a contested self and identity. I try to fit in and act American with my American colleagues, students, neighbours, my children's schoolteachers, and store clerks. At the same time, I proclaim my ethnicity when the occasion demands it. I am Indian American, but how much Indianness do I have left in me and how much can I reproduce? How American should I be, and how much will I be allowed to become? While I attempt to conform to American mainstream culture, I also wear my ethnicity on my sleeve, celebrating Diwali annually with lamps lit on my doorstep, and a presentation on the meaning of Diwali in my sons' school. On the other hand, I do set up a Christmas tree in my home every year. Though I favour pasta and sandwiches for lunch, I often prepare Indian curries and tandoors for dinner. My radio is often set to National Public Radio, but it is equally frequently set to the local Indian station. I am an enormous fan of Bollywood movies and Indian writers who write in English. At the same time, not surprisingly, many of my favourite authors are native-born American and English writers. Equally, my husband and I make it a point to occasionally take our children to see American movies of their choice. My closet is full of not only shirts, jeans, and dresses, but also salwar kameezes and saris. Situated betwixt and between disparate cultures, I am a member of the deterritorialized floating Indian American diaspora that has successfully constructed cross-border transnational identities with the help of regular inflows of people, goods, media images, and ideas from India, and I can certainly identify with the cultural discourses Appadurai has discussed in his works (1996b).

As is clear from the above, diasporic Indian ethnicity is not my only social identity. Like all individuals, I am located in multiple positions of social peripherality as well as centrality. I may project my diasporic identity actively, but I am also conscious of being a Brown immigrant. I did not think of myself as Brown until I came to the West. Essentialization (sometimes positive, but more often pejorative) is a common experience of minority immigrants in the West (Espiritu 2003), and I am no exception. However, in India, my Westernized education, my upper caste status, my ancestral roots in eastern India, and my gender, were the more significant markers of my identity than the colour of my skin.

I arrived in America almost two decades ago. I still remember the thrill I experienced when my flight from Mumbai touched down in Los Angeles International Airport; I had arrived in the United States of America! Soon after, I began to decipher the intricacies of the American accent, local currency, and American traffic rules. Still later, I learned to drive on American roads; it was such fun to drive to the mall and shop for American consumer goods that were out of my reach in my hometown in India. My proudest moments were when I furthered my dream of professional achievement in an academically-rigorous American university environment. I know I am carrying the weight of the academic aspirations of my entire extended family as I progress in my academic career.

Resident in California since the mid-1990s, the racial diversity of California has prompted me to define myself in racial terms. My own 'brownness' came to me reflected in the behaviour of those around me. Hall reminds us that identity is 'always constructed though splitting, splitting between that which one is, and the other'. Thus the self is defined by one's own vantage point, but it is also narrated from the position of the other. The self is 'inscribed in the gaze of the other' (Hall 1997: 48). In many instances, noticing Americans articulating their words over-carefully when they spoke to me, I understood that they were not sure that I comprehended their American accent. A couple of years ago I went to City Hall to attend my naturalization ceremony. There I saw a sea of immigrants of diverse races and ethnicities standing around me, and I was one of them. Gradually I came to confront my own 'brownness'. I began to identify myself as a Brown woman.

Every time I show my US passport to immigration officials, I remember that I am no longer a sojourner, I am an immigrant, here to stay on in the US. My knowledge that I am here in America for good makes it difficult to complain about any real or perceived racism or class bias in the US, for I know that it is my choice to stay on in this country. Stuart Hall has written that identities are never complete, they are never finished: 'Identity is always in the process of formation' (1997: 47) and this has certainly proved to be true in my own life. I identified myself as a highly-educated, upper-caste, eastern Indian woman when I resided in India. But I now see myself as a 'female minority immigrant' and as a 'global multicultural transnational woman'. I know many separate worlds and I can function in all of them, but

I am not sure that I am an 'insider' in any of them. In this work I have analysed women who found themselves within similar intersections of nationality, employment, home, and class affiliations. I am hopeful that my analysis of how immigration, race, gender, class, and employment impact the experience of self and identity of Indian immigrant working women in the San Francisco Bay Area will be useful to future students of gender and migration.

University of California San Diego   ASHIDHARA DAS

Acknowledgements

I WOULD LIKE to express my appreciation to the faculty in the Department of Anthropology at University of California San Diego (UCSD) for the wonderful opportunity they have given me to study there. Professor F.G. Bailey has been instrumental in shaping my theories from the very inception of my studies at the department, and I am deeply grateful for his timely advice, generous encouragement, and invaluable critical insight throughout the process of writing this volume. I have been extremely fortunate to have been his student. I thank Professor Tanya Luhrmann for her inspiring leadership and consistent academic support. Professor Suzanne Brenner guided me through much of this project; her continuing encouragement enabled me to complete my Ph.D. I will always be thankful for her exemplary patience, flexibility, and sustained interest in my research. Professor Yen Le Espiritu's detailed and enlightening comments have been of invaluable assistance in directing my research. Professor Rosemary George's helpful suggestions have improved my study to a great extent. I have drawn extensively on the work and ideas of all my committee members, and I thank them for their faith in my ability to finish this volume. I would also like to extend my appreciation to J.C. Krause and Jed Schlueter, graduate advisors in the department, who played a critical supporting role in this project. In equal measure I am grateful to my teachers at the Department of Sociology in the Delhi School of Economics, University of Delhi, where I completed my Master's degree.

I would like to thank those who commented on the papers I presented at symposia at the UCSD, UC Riverside, and the AAA (American Anthropological Association) conference, etc., at various points of time between 2006 and 2011.

This research work would not have been possible without the generous friendship and willing participation of my subjects who graciously opened their homes to me. I thank them for their openness in relating their lives to me and for taking time out of their hectic schedules to share their views with me. They enabled me to become an active participant observer in their personal and public lives, and I cherish their friendships. My engagement in the social, cultural, and religious network in the Bay Area has enriched my research greatly. The effort to immerse myself in the immigrant community, to understand the segment I chose to study, to look at the life experience of women who were my 'subjects', became a rewarding journey of self-exploration. Hence, I am particularly grateful to those who provided me with field contacts.

I am ever grateful to my father, Professor Sabyasachi Bhattacharya who has been a ceaseless source of inspiration, encouragement and guidance. My deepest gratitude is reserved for my husband Aditya who has provided a bedrock of support. He has always been by my side and his unflagging confidence in my abilities has allowed me to stay the course. My sons Anirban and Ayan have been very understanding with regard to my long absences from home. I am deeply grateful to them for their unconditional love and a maturity far beyond their years. I want to thank my parents-in-law Amita and Pradip Das who have been very supportive in my efforts to successfully complete my research. My mother Malabika Bhattacharya has provided more help than I can describe in words. I cannot thank her enough for the innumerable ways that she has helped me while I was completing this work. It would not have been possible to write this volume without her unflagging nurturing support and commitment to my efforts.

University of California San Diego   ASHIDHARA DAS

CHAPTER I

෴

At Home and at Work in the Diaspora: Theoretical Approaches and a Statistical Overview

INTRODUCTION

THIS RESEARCH WORK focuses on the construction of self and identity by Indian professional and semi-professional women who are resident in the San Francisco-Oakland Bay Area. The objective is to examine how professional achievement and economic mobility can remake gender, race, and class relations for actual ethnographic subjects. Arguably, anthropologists today must be cognizant of sweeping changes in global populations in the current era of late capitalism. Traditionally a study of the 'other' in the colonial and capitalist periphery, anthropology must now adjust to the entrance of the 'other' in unprecedented numbers into the Western core metropolises. Nirmal Puwar and Parvati Raghuram have written about the arrival of difference within the academia (2003), and I here have since been many scholarly works which have focused on the female members of the South Asian diaspora in recent years. There is a burgeoning population of Asian Indians in California. The 2010 Census states that there are 528,176 Asian Indians in California, who constitute 1.4 per cent of the population of the state, and who are especially concentrated in the San Francisco Bay Area. According to the 2010 Census, there are 119,854 Asian Indians in the San Francisco Bay Area, constituting 2.8 per cent of the total population of all the nine counties of the Area. There are a substantial number of working women in this population, many of whom are highly qualified professionals, especially those working in the Silicon Valley.

According to a national survey, 34 per cent of Asian Indian females indicated that they were in professional/managerial occupations (William Darity et al., 'Dressing for Success: Explaining Differences in Economic Performance Among Racial and Ethnographic Groups in the USA', unpublished manuscript, 1994, quoted in Kamala Visweswaran, 1997). The presentation of their negotiation of ethnic difference and monocultural compliance contributes to contemporary debates about gender, work, and migration. While field studies of working class immigrant women have proliferated in recent years, there is a relative absence of empirical research on professional immigrant women who enjoy a measure of socio-economic autonomy. This study will, therefore, be of use to researchers of immigrant relations and employment, and the conclusions will be especially helpful in understanding immigrant dilemmas concerning assimilation, reclamation of ethnic identities, cultural autonomy, and minority agency.

This work addresses the following issues: the various identities and selves of professional Indian women; issues regarding the continuity of the self and identity when individuals constantly shuttle between the starkly different ethnoscapes of the American workplace, and the Indian immigrant home; transnational ideoscapes of belonging; and finally, the ways in which Bay Area Asian Indian women build lives across worlds. Desi is a term used by immigrants from the Indian subcontinent to refer to themselves; it is inclusive of all the diaspora, regardless of their gender, religion, caste, age, or class. A caveat: the research findings reported in this book are specific to the professional class of Indians in the Bay Area, and may not always be applicable to all Indian immigrants.

Undoubtedly the level of assimilation or accommodation vis-à-vis mainstream American society increases with length of residence and employment history in the US, but parallel to this, there is an increasing emphasis on Indian diasporic identity among those who have a long residence experience and employment history. This work argues that the following model explains how these conflicting trends develop in the selves and identities of Asian Indian women in white-collar professions in the Silicon Valley and in other parts of the Bay Area.

The first stage of identity formation takes place in the first couple of years in the US, during which time the women dealt with in this work adapted to the shock of arrival in America. Due to the pervasiveness of Western culture in ex-colonial, neoliberal India, these women had imagined that they were sufficiently familiar with the Western lifestyle to negotiate the intricacies of daily life and culture in America. Though they live in a post-colonial era, they often continue the tradition of emulating Western women, educating themselves in the ways of Westerners, and if possible, immigrating to the West. Seduced by the neoliberal siren song of American global capitalism, they went to the US to pursue the American dream of educational opportunity, technological innovation, and economic prosperity. When they got off the plane from India however, they found that their ignorance of the local linguistic accents, currency, cuisine, fashions, traffic regulations, and modes of behaviour, were sufficiently alienating in the US to make it difficult to function in American society and the workplace. In the first couple of years of living and working in the US, due to the shock of acculturation and Americanization, Asian Indian immigrant women experienced a climactic psychological change similar to an identity crisis. Despite the continuity of an inner ethnic identity, they thought that many of their old social habits, skills, behaviours, and values had become irrelevant in the new situation. The resultant quest to rapidly adopt locally accepted customs, moral standards, and skills can cause considerable internal turmoil.

In the second stage, the women addressed by this work became increasingly familiar with the American way of life. After a couple of years of residence and employment in the US, the Asian Indian women were as comfortable with American linguistic nuances, behavioural codes, cuisine, apparel, and leisure time activities as they were with their Indian counterparts. This made it possible for the women to participate fully in the American workplace, and also in situations outside the workplace. Hence, in this phase, Indian immigrant women became skilled at 'being American'. In this stage, the women were able to completely identify with the host population of the US.

Indian immigrant women who have achieved entry into the current post-industrial, service-related, and technology-based economy in the Bay Area are proud of their professional accomplishments and economic productivity. They are eager to participate in the labour force because their salaries are essential for personal economic empowerment and familial upward mobility. Their professional success also represents the hopes and aspirations of an entire family that wants to move to the West. Employment not only assists in fulfilling visa requirements but also implies freedom from domestic duties and a breaking out from restrictive patriarchal conventions. Employment enables a partial renegotiation of gender relations and a move towards democratization in the Indian immigrant family structure. It facilitates connective female autonomy, that is, the ability to maintain ties with, and even assist the woman's natal family. Married Asian Indian women in the US find it difficult to visit their parents or siblings back in India if they don't earn enough to pay for the US-India flight. As far as housework and childcare are concerned, these women were not very successful in bringing about a more equitable redistribution of domestic responsibilities, but they were able to achieve a major of economic freedom, the corollary of paid employment and aggressive consumerism was their path to class mobility. These women and their families have achieved a version of the 'American dream', and it is because of them, and others like them, that Indian immigrants in the San Francisco Bay Area have become something of a model minority. For example, 41.22 per cent of the housing units occupied by Indians in the Bay Area are owner occupied. The median Asian Indian household income was $88,540, and 47.93 per cent of Asian Indians resident in the Bay Area have a degree that is equivalent to, or higher than a Bachelor's degree. However, employment in professional or white-collar positions does not automatically guarantee good living and advancement opportunities for these women. While some of the women interviewed for this work have reached mid-management positions, many others are stagnating in low grade technical or service positions.

Workplace interaction increases opportunities for assimilation and Indian immigrants use it to train themselves in American ways in order to 'fit in' with their co-workers and supervisors. As the immigrant enters the second stage, the positive psychological effects of joining the American workforce begin to be felt: first, the Asian Indian working women have more opportunity to acculturate into mainstream American culture, and second, the independent identity formation of Indian immigrant career-women is aided by the emphasis on male-female equality in the workplace. Though this emphasis may be superficial, even the rhetoric of workplace gender equity can make a positive psychological impact.

However, this quintessential American success story conceals the psychic costs of uneasy Americanization, social misrecognition, gender battles, and the incessant transnational journeys of the self and of identities. The dominant ethnicity, that is, the Caucasian Americans, sometimes help, but more often divert or resist cultural change in America. Hence, immigrant women often had to disguise their 'difference' if they wish to claim a right to 'equality' in everyday America, and especially in the workplace. By practicing selective inclusion, the dominant majorities include ethnic minorities in spaces where there is an economic need for them, but not in social contexts.

In the third stage, immigrants who have been resident in the US for more than a decade, and who have had prolonged interaction with 'mainstream' Americans, appear to be sceptical of effective assimilation. Many of those interviewed who had been resident for more than decade, felt that irrespective of age, occupation, financial status, or general abilities, individuals of Asian Indian origin, are primarily viewed by 'mainstream' Americans as culturally inassimilable immigrants, or at best, as 'model minorities'. A substantial proportion of them earn middle class level salaries and own well-kept homes, but even after a decade of living in the US, most of them felt that they had not been able to circumvent cultural essentialization in the US. Americanization does increase with length of residence in the US and duration of participation in the American labour force. However, the women in this study reported that despite concerted attempts at being 'American', they continued to be viewed as Asian Indians, that is, as representatives of a foreign culture. Essentialization, whether positive or pejorative, causes psychological dissonance. They were discomfited by the fact that they were called upon to speak for Indian culture precisely when they had begun to drift away from their former Indian habits, and started to adopt new American ways. However, due to their perception that Americans saw them mainly as Indian immigrants, and not as integrated Americans, they embraced the role of being the ethnic representatives of India.

Increased exposure to non-Indians in the workplace has hastened the realization that Asian Indian immigrants are unlikely to ever be completely accepted as 'one of us' by the American population. Immigrant writers who prescribe assimilation as the proper destination of immigrants overlook the fact that for ethnic minorities in the US, assimilation into the mainstream is possible only as a minority. There are of course, other reasons for the attachment to 'Indianness' and the return to Indian culture, the most significant of which was nostalgia. Indianness is a long held identity, and it is also a way to make connections between older and younger generations.

Indian ethnicity provides a convenient hook up on which to hang one's identity. A return to Indian ethnicity bolsters the self and identity, and this is not perceived to contradict the formation of an American identity. Indians in the US feel that a strategic (though partial) reactivation of Indian ethnicity will help them to rise in the race/class hierarchies of the US, and will also allow them to stay within the 'model minority' position. There are reasons to believe that the reproduction of Indian ethnicity abroad also has a subconscious agenda: the aim of trying to show the supposed superiority of Indian spirituality, moral standards, and historical heritage. It is also probable that Indians in the US accentuate their ethnicity to distinguish themselves from other racial and ethnic minorities such as Hispanics and Blacks. All these factors can be seen to account for the reassertion of Indian ethnic identity in the US by those who have been resident in America for a long period of time.

In this context, the Indian immigrant home becomes a principal site for the recomposition of Indian culture. Since Indian women are usually viewed as repositories and transmitters of traditional ethnic culture, the female performance of Indian culture at home is greatly appreciated by Indian immigrant men and by the Indian immigrant community as a whole. The tendency to be Indian at home and as American as possible in the work context manifests itself among the women in this work. The conflicting expectations between the career-oriented woman in the American workforce on one hand, and that of the traditional Indian housewife on the other, create considerable dissonance in the psyche of Asian Indian immigrant women. Also, Indianness at home means, among other things, a return to the inequitable patriarchal relations that characterize the traditional Indian family. This inequity at home is difficult to accept for Indian immigrant women who aspire to be treated as equals of men in their place of work.

The performance of recursive Indian identity also leads to the strengthening of transnational ties to the home country and cross-border loyalties. The recent proliferation in flows of ideas, people, goods, images, and technology in the post-national political world of today has facilitated the activation and maintenance of a diasporic identity. The outcome of this has been the partial abandonment of the path to assimilation, and hence, it results in the reproduction of a diasporic Indian identity that can be activated whenever needed. Asian Indians in the US want to hold on to their lives in the US, but they also desire a 'home away from home'. They plan to retain their diasporic residence and employment, but they also indulge in transnational imaginings of a partial but triumphant return to their 'homeland' where they will feel at home whilst having the financial advantage of an income in dollars. Immigration is no longer a one-way process but the creation of dual lives across national borders. America represents economic riches and individual liberty, while India represents the emotional comfort of living in one's own homeland. In desiring both, they were chasing goals that are worlds apart.

Indian immigrant professional women in the San Francisco Bay Area avail themselves of the burgeoning Indian diasporic cultural resources in their areas by hiring local immigrant producers and teachers of Indian culture. This enables such women to fulfil their perceived obligation to 'enculturate' their offspring in Indian modes of behaviour even while they are at work. In the midst of these developments, they continued to sustain dual contesting identities. Constantly code-switching back and forth between the performance of their American and Indian identities, they formulated a unique response to the contradictions between expectations in the American workplace on the one hand, and the Indian immigrant home on the other.

Comparative analysis searches for variance in experience across different groups. While this work mainly focuses on Indian working women in the US, I have also interviewed settled non-working Indian women resident in the Bay Area, and professional and semi-professional women resident in India. My purpose was to find out the behavioural differences, or lack thereof, made both by participation in the American workplace, and residence in India.

Being largely confined to the home, non-working expatriate Indian women are effectively insulated from American society, hence, their level of Americanization is low. Surprisingly however, such women also exhibit very little identification with the culture and values of present-day India. The majority of the non-working immigrant women appear to live in a time warp for they still tend to function according to the culture of the India they had emigrated from, the India of two or three decades ago. It is probable that the inner psyche of these women becomes very defensive regarding their constant efforts to act against Americanizing peer influences as far as raising their children is concerned. They have to justify their continuing attempts to

Indianize their offspring by denigrating American culture, and also, they have to justify their lack of contribution to household income by excelling in household tasks. Their external self is reflective of the tightly knit community in the midst of which they have found shelter: that of fellow Indian immigrant wives who are not employed.

THEORETICAL FOUNDATIONS

In this section, the theoretical concepts used in this study of the selves and identities of Indian professional and semi-professional working women in the San Francisco Bay Area will be discussed.

Theories of Transnationalism, Globalization, and Diaspora

Arjun Appadurai suggests that due to the current and constant flows of ideas, people, goods, images, and technologies, stable structures such as nation-states are now under threat. Floating diaspora, mobile images and technologies, and cross-border transnational politics disturb the organized form of the nation and the international system, hence the nation-state is no longer the arbiter of modern globality. The authority of the nation-state is challenged by the recent high-volume traffic of people, goods, media, ideas, scientific techniques, and political loyalties across international borders. Such motion is not spatially uniform because ideologies, techniques, messages, populations, and objects are at disjuncture with each other. While some regions may experience the entrance of advanced technological knowledge, alien media images, new liberalizing ideologies, low-level employment positions, and over-priced multinational goods. Other areas however, may be transformed by a deluge of job-hungry inassimilable immigrants from distant homelands, and the import of cheap foreign products of inferior quality. This lack of uniformity causes inequity and suffering in various parts of the world.

Reacting to Benedict Anderson's foundational work on imagined communities, Appadurai reminds us that the imagination emancipates; so where day-to-day struggles result in oppression, the imagination can create a post-national political world. Diasporic public spheres are able to flourish in the interstices between nation-states because electronic mass media eliminates the necessity for face to face interactions. It does away with the need to read and write, or even to understand the language of the region in which a diaspora resides. Thus it is able to link performers and audiences across borders. Electronic personal media facilitates long-distance discussions between complete strangers and enables conversations between friends and relatives even when they are separated by thousands of miles. Imagination, aided by new technology, has given rise to an international civil society, and to mobile global forms of civic life in which nations are but individual transit points (Appadurai 1996b).

Deterritorialization has meant the transportation of both skilled as well as semi-skilled workers from the developing world into wealthy nations where they are likely to occupy lower-class positions. College graduates (especially those who have graduated with the social science degrees) emigrate from India with the help of more qualified family members and frequently resort to working as nannies, food-handlers, caterers, or store clerks in the US. Sometimes they find work as preschool teachers, or substitute schoolteachers, still earning minimum wage for their efforts. Sons of wealthy landholding farmers in India immigrate to the US through legal or illegal means and often find themselves working as cab-drivers, security guards, waiters, or janitors. Sometimes they get work as car-mechanics, or they are able to save or borrow enough money to lease a store-space and run an Indian grocery store, or gas station, or motel. They lead a hand-to-mouth existence. This dislocation of place, political attachment, and class position produces an intensified attachment to the culture left behind in the country of origin. Appadurai uses the example of Islam, which functions outside national boundaries and goals due to the dedicated activities of overseas believers. He also writes of how the cultural reproduction of Hinduism by Indian immigrants abroad has been tied to Hindu fundamentalism at home. The persistence of multicultural debates in Europe and the US is a 'testimony to the incapacity of states to prevent their minority populations from linking themselves to wider constituencies of religious or ethnic affiliation'. Thus, we cannot assume any longer that all or most 'viable public spheres' are national and instead of national public spheres, we now have a post-national order of diasporic public spheres. 'Diasporic public spheres, diverse among themselves, are the crucibles of a post-national political order. The engines of their discourse are mass media (both interactive and expressive) and the movements of refugees, activists, students, and labourers' (1996b: 23).

In general, Appadurai's formulations are useful, but as Aihwa Ong has pointed out, they are open to criticism on account of his failure to locate the imagination as a social process within the national politico-economic structures that control the flows of people, ideas, technology, goods, images, and finances. In addition, Appadurai's formulations do not consider class stratifications in the global economy. Rather, he gives the impression that global capitalism is liberating for all, when in fact, it mainly benefits the global elite. This global elite is substantially regulated by states that have fashioned a new relationship to capital mobility and manipulations through flexible citizens and non-citizens (1999).

Despite the lacunae in his theories, Appadurai's conceptions remain useful, for they move the reader away from earlier linear theories of immigration where the immigrant is only imagined to move from arrival to assimilation to nationhood. Appadurai's theory of transnationalism is useful in its multilinear and multitemporal formulation, for it creates a space for the immigrant to be re-imagined. To understand how progressive Appadurai's theory is, it is useful to examine some older influential American theories of immigration. Writing just before the new wave of immigrants entered the US in the 1960s, Moynihan and Glazer wrote of different immigrant groups in their popular book *Beyond the Melting Pot* (1963). They identified Catholics, Jews, white Protestants, and Negroes as the principal groups which comprise the American people. This formulation seems outdated in modern times, but many of the theories of Moynihan and Glazer have aged better. For example, they claimed that race and religion constitute two salient paradigms in the organization of the American population. Rejecting the notion that America is a 'melting pot' in which incoming immigrants assimilate completely, Moynihan and Glazer held that plural ethnicities had survived American conditions, and that they would continue to do so. Milton Gordon's influential work *Assimilation in American Life* (1964) was published just a year after Moynihan and Glazer's work, and he too, perceived race and religion to be the two main organizing principles of the diverse subcultures and sub-societies in America.

Many of the social trends beginning to emerge at the time when Glazer, Moynihan, and Gordon were formulating their theories gathered momentum after the publication of their works and in the context in which they were produced. In the mid-1960s, the Black civil rights movement demanded racial integration. However, by the late 1960s, ideas of Black power, Black pride, and Black ethnic unity that were ambivalent over whether racial desegregation was preferable to racial separation (accompanied by ethnic vitality) at the cost of ethnic dissolution began to be visible in American society. Led by their example, native Indians, Chicanos, and White groups also initiated a resurgence and reclamation of their ethnic identities. Group interests such as native Indian tribal autonomy, or Black community control over schools that had a Black student majority, motivated many ethnic revivalist movements.

From the 1960s onwards, and especially in the 1990s, millions of new immigrants from Asia and Latin America settled in the US. Building on the civil rights won by the social activists of the 1960s, the new immigrants have actively worked for linguistic, cultural, and religious perpetuation of their own ethnic groups within the US.

All these developments in pluralist America bring us to an important question: How far should a nation-state allow pluralism to develop? The American nation is premised on the ethics of democratic individualism and liberal pluralism. With the exception of the prevention of discrimination, liberal pluralism does not envisage the state as a direct controller of race and ethnic relations. It is committed to providing equal opportunities for all individuals, but it does not concern itself with the structural position or cultural uniqueness of ethnic groups. The state advocates tolerance for the protection of cultural distinctiveness, but it assumes a willingness to assimilate enough to identify with the national democratic goal of maintaining national unity, whilst allowing for the coexistence of different ethnic groups.

When ethnic and racial corporations obtain legal, political, and economic powers such that they can restrict the educational, occupational, associational, residential, franchise, and linguistic rights and facilities of individuals on the basis of whether or not they are part of the ethnic group, then democratic universalism and identification with national values, ideas, and institutions come under threat. Cultural and racial separatism allows ethnic minorities to participate in their distinctive culture to the fullest extent, but it also prevents them from obtaining structural assimilation, thus ultimately cutting them off from civic and political assimilation.

Appadurai writes of this phenomenon, explaining that because of its pluralistic outlook, and because of its pride in being a land of immigrants, the US continues to be the chosen destination for thousands of immigrants every year. The challenge is to balance multiculturalism with national unity. America has a long history of immigration from different parts of the world; the Native Indians are the only people who can truly claim to be native to the US for more than a couple of centuries, everybody else has descended from immigrants who came to the US in the last couple of centuries. Hence, most Americans have hyphenated identities, and their ethnic identities are threatening to overwhelm their American ones. Thus, the notion of the nation is able to grow transnationally, but the legitimacy of the nation-state is under attack within its own territorial region (1996b).

Appadurai stresses that diasporic peoples become more loyal to their nation of origin after having left its often unpleasant realities, hence there are now many 'transnations' in the US. These transnations are thoroughly diasporic, but they are founded on the ideology of putative origin from a common place or nation. In agreement with Appadurai, Madhulika Khandelwal (2002) shows in her research on Indians in the New York metropolitan area that Indian culture is able to be transplanted in the US, for it is so strong that it can easily take root in new soil. It is of course, slightly transformed by the long-haul journey across thousands of miles. Also, just as Indian culture is divided by region, religion, and class, in America too, culture is diversified even within the community by these same factions. The efforts to maintain transnational ties have caused Indian immigrants to become more Indian in America than they were in India itself (Ibid.).

Sandhya Shukla is also in general agreement with Appadurai. She admits that there are substantial transnational flows of finances, social relations, and political ideologies between India the US. However, she also suggests that the heart of diasporic sensibility lies in how Indian migrants have constructed

India as a means to negotiate life in the multicultural US. Rather than a nationalist passion for former homelands, it is in the creation of a symbolic India that Indian immigrants can constitute a post-colonial national identity, and also a space in the developed world of the US. Hence the diasporic formation of Indianness, is more of an imaginary site for group identity in urban and suburban areas of settlement, than an actual territorial state. In today's globalized world, the notion of Indianness provides a discourse for migrant articulation about race, ethnicity, and multiculturalism (2003).

Though America is proud to be a pluralistic and democratic nation of immigrants, no nation, not even the US, can contain such a variety of transnations without facing challenges. 'In today's post-national, diasporic world, America is being invited to weld these two doctrines together, to confront the needs of pluralism *and* of immigration, to construct a society *around* diasporic diversity' (Appadurai 1996b: 172–3).

Appadurai and his adherents present a convincing scenario of transnational 'virtual neighbourhoods' in which ethnoscapes are formed by modern technological mediascapes which in turn aid borderless imaginations. However, such an account of global diasporic imagined communities could be seen to trivialize the permanence of immigrants in their new homes. As Lisa Lowe has shown, the critical flaw in transnational theory is that it places too great an emphasis on cross-border links, and neglects the permanence of immigrant homes in the country of settlement. Whether or not they imagine that they will return home in the end, almost all immigrants end up living their entire lives in the adopted country. Theories of transnationalism fail to account for this reality of cross-border lives (1996).

Theories of transnationalism also fail to give due importance to the issues of race and ethnicity which disrupt and realign everyday life for immigrants. After all, problems of race and racism cannot be wished away by globally linked diasporic imaginations. Howard Winant of the racial formation approach has formulated that race identity, and indeed race itself, is not stable but rather is constantly being politically constructed. Racial formation occurs at the intersection of representation with structures and institutions and these intersections are articulations of the meaning of race. Winant argues that it is impossible and indeed should not be attempted to transcend race, for race is a marker of a long history of both established systems of truth and epochal struggles for freedom, human rights, and solidarity. The legacy of the post Second World War anti-racial movements brought a vision of racial justice, but despite the many racial reforms carried out, the effects of colonial rule, apartheid, and segregation have not yet been overcome (2004).

In addition to these issues, there are a few more questions about transnational identity that need to be addressed. The first revolves around the idea of whether transnational or diasporic identity is meant to further status claims for immigrants, and whether it succeeds in this attempt. After all, even if the ethnic community showers praise on those who excel in ethnic cultural performance, the problem of the host society remains. After all, most mainstream Americans, whether White, Black, or Hispanic, do not understand or appreciate Indian songs, dances, or plays.

The second question is concerned with the emphasis on the transnational recreation of Indian sensibilities in the diaspora and whether they replicate inequitable gender and caste discriminations in the country of settlement. It has been widely recognized that unjust gender relations are indeed reproduced in America in an attempt to bring about ethnic resurgence (George 2005; Espiritu 2003; Dasgupta 1998; Agarwal 1991). In her analysis of Filipino immigrants, Espiritu has shown that since immigrant communities perceive that the dominant ethnic group views them as different and hence non-normative, the immigrant community attempts to claim moral superiority over the dominant community by becoming hyper-vigilant in forbidding women from indulging in what it believes to be transgressions of female virtue. This process further reinforces patriarchy within the overseas community (2003).

The third question addresses the issue of the authenticity of the ethnic culture produced and performed in the diaspora. There are of course issues surrounding the concept of authenticity, since all cultures are always under production and formation. Some scholars have justifiably raised the issue of whether Indian immigrants in America could have their own culture at all, even if it is different from that of both their homeland and their adopted country. While this is a valid objection to the insistence on authenticity, we cannot ignore Shamita Dasgupta's observation that the contradictions and intricacies that emerge in a lived culture, as in the Indian homeland, are obliterated deliberately in the US, in the name of 'unity, coherence, and formal presentation to the dominant mainstream' (1998: 5). Many scholars have shown that transnational practitioners of their native culture are outdated (Mazumdar 1996), for they cross-identify and code-switch too often to do any justice to either the culture of the homeland or the host country. T.M. Luhrmann has suggested that an authentic self is difficult to achieve especially for post-colonial subjects since such individuals are steeped in a history of cross-identification and rejection (1996). The same is even more applicable for post-colonial immigrants who leave their homeland for more prosperous nations.

Vijay Prashad has provided a partial response to the issues discussed here in that he explains that it is due to the racist rejection by the host society, that desis accept the only space sanctioned by US society: a hyper-Indian 'orientalist' ethnic space. Seen as superior to 'Americans' in terms of spiritual matters but inferior in terms of practical matters, Indian immigrants attempt to find at least an intermediary place in the race hierarchy. They obtain a position which is seen to be inferior to Whites but superior to Blacks. Hence, in order to maintain at least this marginal position of superiority, Indian immigrants tend to embrace the 'model minority' image and in many instances, they even resort to anti-Black racist chauvinism. Prashad urges Indians in the US to reject this racial contract, and to renegotiate solidarity with all of the oppressed races in America (2000). Indian ethnic identity has been resurrected in the US due to social rejection and the desire to get ahead in multiracial America. Ultimately however, it transforms into a transnational and diasporic identity which attempts to escape the compulsions of colour lines in the US by imagining a global Indian or global South Asian mobile community.

Aihwa Ong has resolved some related questions in her interesting study of transnational elite Chinese investors and traders. Ong finds that the ethno-racial moral order of the host community lessens ability of the transnationals to transform economic capital into social advantage, and also that gender relations in transnational families are regulated by family regimes that usually validate male mobility, and idealize female localization. Cultural norms favour global mobility for peripatetic Chinese males, enabling them to accumulate capital and power, but it disciplines women and children, forcing them to live restricted and stationary lives. As far as authenticity of identity is concerned, Ong points out that among transnational individuals, personal identity seldom coincides with state-imposed identity. The global economy of the current late capitalist period has motivated many Chinese people to invest outside and to immigrate to economically gainful and politically secure 'safe haven' destinations outside the home nation. Despite obtaining citizenship in far away nations, such voluntarily displaced persons tend to retain their personal Chinese identity. Thus, the Chinese transnational is able to adroitly navigate the demands of family, state, and capital, all the while being true to his ethnic transnational practices and imaginings. However, Ong cautions that these manipulations only articulate the tension between the state and global capital, they do not herald the end of the nation-state or a 'clash of civilizations' (1999).

Theories of Immigration

In his groundbreaking study *Strangers from a Different Shore,* Ronald Takaki argues that European and Asian immigrants alike came to the US for a fresh start. A third generation Asian American himself, Takaki focuses on the 'long hours of labour and racial discrimination' which the Asian Americans had to endure in the US in the 1800s and early 1900s. Takaki concludes that, 'they [Asian immigrants] did not permit exterior demands to determine wholly the direction and quality of their lives. Energies pent up in the old countries were unleashed, and they found themselves pursuing urges and doing things they had thought beyond their capabilities' (1989: 18). These immigrants wanted to become part of the American dream, but, as Takaki complains, to this day, there is a perpetual lack of acceptance of Asian Americans by other Americans even if the former have lived in the US for several generations.

In a study conducted some years ago among Indian immigrants resident in the UK, Rashmi Desai found a similar lack of acceptance of Indian immigrants into the social life of the British majority. Desai showed that this resulted in a reluctance to assimilate on the part of Indians in the UK. In his survey completed in the 1960s, Rashmi Desai examined both blue- and white-collar workers in UK and found that in both groups, there was a sense that immigrants were left out of British social networks, and if they were integrated, they were granted only an inferior status. Hence, there was an overwhelming tendency among his interviewees to confine their social interaction to other Indian immigrants. In Desai's time, immigration was encouraged by the presence of sponsors who were usually fellow villagers from India, or relatives, and they formed the foundation of the immigrant community due to their initial economic stability. This allowed junior relatives or village kin to act as a source of extra income for their families in India, and a supplementary source of labour in the UK. This pattern of immigration resulted in an extremely close-knit Indian community, for there were large groups of immigrants who were related by blood or marriage, and were very often from the same village in India. This immigrant population was largely male as wives and children tended to be left behind in India (1963).

While residential, leisure, and companionship needs were met by the internal social circuit of these immigrants, it was the idea of work or economic function which was the primary objective of the passage to the UK and this was only obtainable externally. Thus, the immigrant had to venture into the host society in order to earn a living. Desai writes that work-related interactions with members of the host society led to 'single-stranded relationships'. For example, Indian immigrants met their British co-workers in the factory every day, but the initial relationship rarely grew further.

Indian immigrants were integrated into the British workforce and were a part of the British labour unions, but they did not assimilate into wider society since their interactions were confined largely to professional and labour associated functions. The immigrant group as a whole could therefore be considered as largely 'accommodating', rather than 'assimilating'.

Desai wrote that integration related to assimilation sees immigrants coming to share the attitudes, values, and behaviours of the host society with which they identify themselves. In contrast, in the process of 'accommodation', immigrants typically accept the relationships available to them and act with some degree of conformity, even though they do not share the bulk of attitudes and values which are part of the host society. Assimilation participation extends far beyond the work situation into a domain where social behaviour is based on acculturation to the host society, whereas accommodation participation is restricted to the work environment. Desai found that Indian immigrants in the UK largely accommodated toward their environment and tried to avoid assimilation.

Desai's study has been useful to me not only for its theoretical insights, but also because it has provided me with an historical point of comparison between present-day Indian immigrants in the US and Desai's subjects. My comparison with Desai's data from the 1960s in the UK shows that the current pattern of immigration in America is different. Desai's subjects were mostly brought to the UK by senior relatives and older village kin who needed a second income or some assisance in running a business in the UK. However, this type of migration is the exception, rather than the rule in present-day America. Thus, unlike Desai's mostly male labourers and clerks who had been sponsored by village kin or relatives, the Asian Indian population in the US is largely composed of highly educated and qualified men and women who have been invited to study or work in universities, corporations, and other institutions such as hospitals, and who are accompanied by their nuclear families. The Luce Bill, brought into effect in 1965, allows the entry of only those Indian immigrants who have secured admission to an American university, or who have been offered employment by an American corporation. The spouse and children of such immigrants are allowed to accompany them on adjunct visas, making them ineligible for employment until such time as permanent resident status (Green Card) is obtained. Such residents have the option of becoming US citizens through the process of naturalization after a period of five years and an Indian immigrant can only help his siblings or parents to migrate to the US after obtaining this citizenship. There is however a significant population of Indian immigrant blue-collar workers in the US whose lives are probably more similar to Desai's immigrants in the UK than to those of the Indian American professional white-collar workers and their families. These groups comprise the labour class remnants of the pre-1965 first wave of Indian immigrants who were semi-skilled and generally less qualified than the post-1965 Luce Bill wave of selected professional immigrants.

Both the skilled workers and labourers of the present-day Indian American immigrant population resemble Desai's Indians in one significant respect: they also pursue social self-segregation. This is a common feature of both categories of Indians currently resident in the US just like those in the UK in the 1960s. Despite differences in patterns of immigration between Desai's subjects and present-day Indian immigrants in America, the two groups have similar social habits. Like Desai's subjects, first generation Indians in the US continue to socialize almost exclusively with co-ethnics (preferably from the same region/linguistic group in India, and of the same economic status). Pockets of high density Indian populations in different parts of America enable regular face-to-face meetings between Indians. Also,

Indian immigrants support co-ethnic economic ventures by patronizing Indian grocery stores, Indian video and DVD rental shops, restaurants, dance and music instructors, Hindu priests, and by pooling money to open new business ventures such as computer software start-up companies. These are new forms of the entrepreneurial activities within the internal Indian immigrant economy which Desai was exploring in the 1960s.

Desai concluded that while his subjects had accommodated to British life, they had not assimilated to it. The same is true of first generation Indian immigrants who have recently arrived or who have been resident in the US for a decade or less. The social circulation of these immigrants is confined to their own ethnic/linguistic unit. As a whole, the group accepts unfamiliar social practices by the host society, since it has no option but to do so but it also hopes that its own unique ethnic behaviours will be tolerated by the host community. Superficial changes are made in dress, diet, and financial habits in order to conform to some of the minimum requirements of the host society. Despite this, in general neither group nor individual US resident Indian immigrants identify socially or culturally with the host citizenry, hence assimilation is minimal.

However, my research found that unlike Desai's subjects, after several decades of living in America, my interviewees experienced gradual internal Americanization. Their self-identity and sensibilities became more and more American and in the end, they bore little resemblance to the family and friends they had left behind in India. Contrary to this, this stage is also characterized by a concerted effort to maintain Indianness in limited aspects of life, such as religious rituals, food and dress on special occasions such as weddings, births, and funerals. There is also an effort to provide Indian cultural training to the children, and the self-segregation of Indian ethnics continues.

While Desai explained that a lack of social welcome by the host society had discouraged Indian immigrants in UK from venturing into the British mainstream, all white-collar workers in the Bay Area reported that the Americans they came in contact with were polite and seldom cold or hostile. However, native-born Americans seldom welcomed immigrant outsiders into their social cliques and my subjects preferred to interact with fellow Indians because they felt more comfortable with them. Naturally, this tendency to stay within the Indian community prevented immigrants from identifying fully with the American mainstream. Equally, many of my interviewees said that they preferred to think of themselves as part of a global Indian diaspora, 'comfortable in any cosmopolitan city of the world' (as one of my interviewees said), rather than envisage themselves as minorities in the American nation.

Harry H.L. Kitano and Roger Daniels express the immigrant dilemma aptly in the following passage:

Who wants to become an American? The apparently simple question turns out to be difficult and complicated, since it involves different 'Americas'. If becoming an American means full acceptance and the chance for equal participation in the mainstream, most immigrants would answer with a resounding YES. If becoming American means giving up ones cultural heritage in order to participate in the mainstream, the affirmative response of some immigrants might have a lowered intensity. If it means discrimination and a second-class role, then some immigrants would not wish to become Americans. (1988: 4)

THEORIES OF GENDER, WORK, AND IMMIGRATION

Immigrant women experience adjustment problems in a far greater degree than their male counterparts. Sangeeta Gupta explains:

I believe that gender role expectations from South Asian cultures along with the mainstream Western culture form the foundations of their various struggles. Thus, expectations affect various generations of women in different ways. While first generation parents want their children to adopt some aspects of Western culture such as education or occupation (what we may call structural assimilation), they also expect their offspring to shed this 'foreign' influence at will under other circumstances (especially related to issues surrounding dating and marriage). Thus parents do not want their children to completely submerge themselves in this mainstream culture by adopting all Western social patterns of behaviour, referred to as cultural assimilation. (1999: 12)

Espiritu has explained that female wage employment reconfigures patriarchal relations in immigrant families. Racialization diminishes male employability in the country of settlement and though female immigrants also experience racism, along with sexism and sexual harassment, this has not stopped them from obtaining and retaining employment. As far as professional women are concerned, just like women in other occupational positions, they are burdened by full-time workloads as well as by housework and childcare. Hence, they have had to confront their husbands about sharing household labour. Some professionals such as nurses, obstetrical/gynaecologist physicians, and nightshift technical support crew, need significant assistance from their husbands in childcare and so it is often the husbands who drop the children at school in the morning and put them to bed at night. Increased male participation in traditionally female tasks has dealt a blow to male privilege, but women's attempts to bring about more equitable family relations are hemmed in by their need for a double income and their desire for a strong and intact family. There is an over reliance on the family and the ethnic community since these are the main resources in the struggle against racial subordination within the dominant society (1999).

As Sheba Mariam George points out, the person who arrives first is very important within immigrant families. Family members who are primary immigrants sponsor the immigration of other family members to the US and so they are typically the first in their families to become conversant with the ways of the host society. Their spouse and children depend on them considerably during the settlement process. This helps them in the structuring of gender relations to their advantage at home and in the ethnic community. If they continue to be the primary breadwinner, then they retain their advantage over other family members. George has written about female professional immigrant Indian (Keralite) nurses, who migrated before their husbands and also have higher economic status, hence they can enjoy comfortable gender relations at home and in their community (2005). This study is helpful to me since it validates strong belief behind this study, that post-immigration gender configurations depend greatly on the order of arrival and the salaries of male and female members of the immigrant household.

In fact other scholars such as Lamphere also state that the more women earn in comparison to their men, the more empowered they are at home (1993). Hondagneu-Sotelo explains that due to spatial mobility, post-immigration women have greater authority in the family than they had before coming to America, and those who used natal networks to get to America enjoy more equitable gender relations than those who were sponsored by their husband (1994). Rather than a straightforward economic reductionist view however, a more nuanced approach should be adopted in which not just income, but also family solidarity and ethnic pride must be taken into account when analysing the re-structuring of gender relations within the post-immigration family.

In her ethnographically rich study of Indians in New York City, Madhulika Khandelwal writes that Indian immigrants view female full-time employment as a new gender role. Khandelwal affirms that professional Indian women feel that their income in the US gives them a new authority within the household and an exhilarating freedom from economic dependence on their husbands. Indian immigrant men in the US are reported to be apprehensive about losing ground to women in the internal power struggle within the household. Indian immigrant women and men alike share concerns over issues of racism and the glass ceiling, but the women have gender specific complaints about, for example, the lack of support from female relatives or of domestic servants, a resource that is commonly available in India. Also, many college-educated women expressed anger over having been rejected by mainstream sources of employment as they had been forced to find employment in ethnic niches or in the Indian underground economy. Khandelwal's work is significant for it validates many of the research findings of this study regarding work related attitudes, and diasporic gender articulations (2002).

Psychological Theories

Symbolic interactionism, which I will discuss in the following paragraphs, has allowed me to analyse my subjects from both a social and a psychological perspective. The ideas that initiated this school of thought were formulated by intellectual pioneers such as William James, Charles Horton Cooley, and George Herbert Mead.

Mead achieved a transformative breakthrough by developing a theory of the self and the mind that clearly explained how a phase of inner consciousness gives rise to a phase of outer initiation of action. Human beings select particular features of their universe and jointly assign symbols to them in order to communicate shared meanings. This collective reconstruction of the universe enables the organization of diverse individual perspectives into a single group perspective. Thus, individuals are able to respond to each other in the manner in which they expect others to respond to them. Also, individuals find it possible to perform actions that will motivate others to respond in accordance with their expectations. Individual action is a result of both creative impulse as well as reflective consideration. In Mead's formulation, 'I' refers to the initial impulsive phase of attitude and action, whereas 'Me' is the secondary phase and is a result of reflection over the expected reactions of others to the individual initial phase of action. Continual interplay between 'I' and 'Me' indicates an unending cycle of action and evaluation where the 'Me' is led by the 'generalized other', or the internalization of the rules and roles of the social order (1934, 1938).

Almost half a century after Mead, Erving Goffman (1983) made a seminal contribution to symbolic interactionism by urging sociology students to study the 'interaction order'. The 'interaction order' is what transpires in surroundings in which one or more individuals are physically in one another's 'response presence'. Goffman makes a strong case for the study of all socially situated actions in order to understand the forms of social life they derive from, such as relationships, informal groups, age categories, gender, ethnic minorities, and social class. The 'interaction order' refers to social exchanges that are relatively circumscribed in space and most certainly in time—it is ultimately about interactions in the here and now. It is also about a social life that is promissory and evidential, that is, one where others can form conjectures about an individual's intent, status, and relationships from his appearance, manner, and actions. Moreover, the 'interaction order' functions according to social conventions, or ground rules.

While symbolic interactionism has been useful to me for understanding the individual adoption and shedding of different identities in different social situations, the work of Erik Erikson (1963, 1968) has helped me to account for the inner continuity of personality that endures through changes in social situations and life cycle stages. Erikson held that identity is the result of interaction between the inner psychic structure on one hand, and internalization of social norms on the other. Ego identity or individual personality is based on a combination of different group identities such as social heritage and geographical locations.

According to Erikson, there are eight stages in the individual life cycle, each stage being marked by biological, social, and psychological milestones peculiar to the specific stage. Though personality is marked by inner continuity, and is constant irrespective of changes in life stages, the individual is likely to experience a climactic psychological change, called an identity crisis, during adolescence. Difficult circumstances, such as sudden and stark changes in the social and physical environment, might also trigger an identity crisis later in life. Despite such crisis events, in general identity is a constant and continuous sameness of being on account of it being located deep in the psychic structure of the individual.

Some of our subjects and interviewees described their adjustment to their new life in America in terms reminiscent of an 'identity crisis' such as that described by Erikson. Due to climactic psychological changes caused by an immigration-related repositioning of function and status, there are significant shifts in personality. Sameness of being is difficult to maintain upon immigration to a new social, linguistic, political, technological, and national environment. Accustomed to being upper caste, upper middle class members of the Indian religious and socio-economic mainstream, many of my subjects wondered if their new identity in America was bound to be that of a subordinate minority. They also expressed a certain ambivalence about being counted as part of an American minority. Philip Gleason (1992) has shown that since the 1930s, American use of the word 'minority' has led to associating it with victimization. In fact, victimhood has continued to remain a crucial factor in the definition of a minority. The Civil Rights revolution seized upon the word to describe those who had been victimized by American society on account of their race and who were now determined to fight for equality. Minority became a semi-legal term when desegregation took place and affirmative action came into force. However, only those groups that were officially designated as minorities benefited from affirmative action. In general, race and ethnicity, rather than distinctive non-racial characteristics such as religion or culture, are the criteria for entitlement to affirmative action. Therefore, the American minorities that are recipients of affirmative action are mostly people of colour such as African Americans, Native American Indians, Asians and Hispanics.

Asian Indians had been categorized as Caucasians by the US government until 1980. In the 1970s, Asian Indians petitioned to switch their Census designation from the category of White/Caucasian to that of Asian/Pacific Islander. This move was motivated by the desire to be in the category to which they logically belonged, but mostly by the hope of qualifying for affirmative action programmes on account of their 'minority' status. In 1980, Asian Indians were included in the Asian/Pacific Islander group in the Census. Despite their choice to be legally recognized as an American 'minority', Asian Indians are ambivalent about their inclusion among other minorities, for they perceive other minorities such as African Americans and Hispanics as a 'backward' underclass in America. Though such prejudice is difficult to understand, I fear that many Indians in America are reluctant to be grouped and equated together with disadvantaged minority groups. The subjects of this study seemed to prefer to project a diasporic/transnational identity rather than accept a 'backward' minority identity. They wanted to project their ethnicity as a positive social heritage, to be seen as part of a global population of prosperous, highly qualified non-resident Indians who deserve a place in the American middle class. In fact, now that many affirmative action measures are no longer legally enforced, Indian Americans see little value in being classified among underprivileged 'minorities'. Some Indians in the US aspire to follow the Jewish model in that they want to gain prominence through educational, financial, and political success, and eventually to influence US government policies proactively just as Jewish Americans have done.

This study postulates that in the first few years of residence and work experience in the US, the subjects undergo an identity crisis. The ego identity of individual personality is based on group identity and social heritage. The group and social environment changes radically when new immigrants first enter a new country. They become especially conscious of this change when they interact with local people at work. Due to the shock of acculturation and Americanization, which pulls against the durability of their ethnic and national consciousness, the subjects all experienced a climactic psychological change. Despite the continuity of inner identity, a perception exists that many, if not most, old social habits, skills, behaviour, and values are irrelevant in the new situation. The resultant venture to rapidly adopt locally accepted customs, moral standards, and skills causes enormous internal strife that lessens only upon successful adjustment to the new environment.

AN HISTORICAL AND STATISTICAL OVERVIEW

Currently there are 2.84 million Asian Indians in the US (2010 US Census Bureau). They reside mainly in the urban areas of the nation and their numbers are highest in the states of California, New York, and New Jersey. Of the 528,176 Indians residing in California (according to the 2010 Census), some are Indian citizens (residing in the US as international students, H-1B visa holders, or Green Card holders) and others are US citizens. The H-1B programme has enabled hundreds of thousands of Indian professionals to live and work in the US. Indian computer professionals, including tens of thousands of techies in the Silicon Valley, benefited greatly from the dot.com boom of 1997 to 2000. When the dot.com industry went into decline in 2001, Indian professionals found it difficult to hold on to their privileged position in the job market. In the Bay Area, large numbers of computer and other professionals were made redundant and this had a devastating impact on the Indian community. Out of work, and consequently out of visa status, many Indians on H-1B visas were forced to choose between going back home with their meagre savings, or staying on in the US illegally. In 2012, with the American economy recovering from a long economic recession, Bay Area high-tech industries are beginning to come into their own again. Due to this, the Indian community in the Bay Area is prospering on the whole, though many are returning to the riches of the currently shining Indian economy.

THE IMMIGRATION REFORM OF THE 1960s

The Hart-Cellar Immigration Act of 1965 was a landmark in the immigration history of the US. The national origin system was ended and highly qualified professionals were favoured in the new system. At the time when the Hart-Cellar Immigration Act was passed, Asian immigrants constituted only 0.05 per cent of the US population, but according to the 2010 Census, Asian immigrants currently make up as much as 4.8 per cent of the American population.

TABLE 1.1 Race and Ethnicity in the US

Race	Percentage of total US population	Change 2000–10
White	72.4	5.7+
Black or African American	12.6	12.3+
Indian American and Alaskan Native	0.9	18.4+
Asian	4.8	43.3+
Native Hawaiian and other Pacific islander	0.2	35.4+
Some other race	6.2	24.4+
Two or more races	2.9	32.0+
Hispanic or Latino	16.3	43.0+

SOURCE: 2010 Census as shown in *www.census.gov*

Taking advantage of the new immigration regulations, hundreds of thousands of Indian professionals immigrated to the US in the 1970s, 1980s, and 1990s. The post-1965 wave of immigrants from India mostly consisted of highly educated and skilled professionals. They came on H-1B visas which enabled them to reside and work in the US for six years. After six years, they could apply for a Green Card. Once they obtained the Green Card, they became eligible to apply for citizenship after five years. Many other Indians entered the US as students on F1 visas which allowed them to study in the US for a total of six years. Unlike the earlier Indian immigrants, the new Indian immigrants were able to bring their wives and children with them. While the majority of the early immigrants were from the state of Punjab, post-1965 Indian immigrants were from various different regions of India. Being professionals, they favoured the job opportunities available in urban areas and so they rarely settled in rural regions. Equally, preferring to pursue the American middle class dream of buying a house in urban areas or in the suburbs nearing big cities, post-1965 Indian immigrants did not usually settle in ethnic enclaves.

TABLE 1.2 Total Number of Asian Indians in the US

Year	Total number of Asian Indians
1980	361,531
1990	815,447
2000	1,678,785
2010	2,843,391

SOURCE: Manju Sheth 1997: 32, INS, and US Census data.

While middle class, well-educated, urbanized professionals constituted the bulk of Indian immigrants who came to the US in the late 1960s and 1970s, the less educated, less qualified relatives (parents and siblings) of the post-1965 Indian immigrants began arriving in the US by the 1980s. Their visas were approved under the 'family reunification preference' categories. For example, 65 per cent of Indian immigrants who arrived in the US before 1980 had a Bachelor's degree or higher, but only 53 per cent of the Indian immigrants who came to the US between 1980 and 1990 had obtained education of equal standing (Gupta 1999: 15). Unable to find professional employment, most of these newcomers set up small businesses such as motels, grocery stores, and restaurants in the US.

The 1990s however, witnessed an upsurge of skilled computer professionals emigrating from India: American firms hired them to solve Y2K problems and to work on other current projects (the Y2K problem, or the Year 2000 problem, was a predicament for computer-related and other documentation and data storage systems; due to the tradition of abbreviating a four-digit year to two digits, there was widespread apprehension that long-working computer systems would break down when the year 1999 would roll over into 2000). By the late 1990s, more than a 100,000 overseas workers arrived annually in the US. The 2000 Census counted approximately 400,000 H-1B visa holders in the US and during the peak of the dot.com boom, i.e. between October

1999 and February 2000, Indians received 43 per cent of all H-1B visas issued by the Immigration and Naturalization Services Agency (INS Documents). The Bay Area has been a magnet for H-1B visa holders, many of whom are Indian, to the point that in 2000, the Bay Area accounted for as much as 12 per cent of nationwide applications to obtain H-1B visa holders. This figure seems particularly high when keeping in mind that the population of this area constitutes only 2 per cent of the total population of the US. At 19.89 and 12.23 per cent respectively, California and New York were the two states which accounted for the highest percentages of applications for H-1B visas.

Shambhu Rao, executive director of the Indo-American Community Services Centre, witnessed the enormous increase in the number of Indian immigrants in the Bay Area first-hand. Rao's Santa Clara centre provided services such as counselling, yoga, and personal computer education classes. In an interview in 2001, he explained that the clientele coming to his centre for classes had increased dramatically over the last few years. Even the influx of older persons had increased: 'We used to have 25 to 30 senior citizens that would come in the daytime, now we are getting 100 a day.' The swelling immigrant populace was made up not only of primary immigrants and their wives and children, but also of the siblings and parents of primary immigrants. As for these primary immigrants, Rao estimated that about 30,000 Indian H-1B visa holders came into the Bay Area for high-tech jobs in the late 1990s. Rao states that, 'There weren't enough qualified people in the US. That's why they went and got people from India and China, and Indians have a slight advantage because many of them can speak English.' (*San Francisco Chronicle*, 16 May 2001).

TABLE 1.3 Racial and Ethnic Diversity in the San Francisco Bay Area

Race and ethnicity	Population	Percentage of total population
White	3,755,823	52.5
Black or African American	481,361	6.7
Indian American and Alaskan Native	48,493	0.7
Asian	*1,664,384*	*23.3*
Native Hawaiian and other Pacific islander	44,386	0.6
Some other race	770,820	10.8
Two or more races	385,472	5.4
TOTAL	7,150,739	100.0
Hispanic or Latino (of any race)	1,681,800	23.5

SOURCE: 2010 Census as shown in *www.census.gov*

TABLE 1.4 A Cross-Section of the Asian Indian Community among 8* Counties of the San Francisco-Oakland Bay Area

San Francisco Bay Area County	Population				Asian Indian having		Median Household Income ($) Asian Indian
	Total of all races	Total Asian Indian	Female Asian Indian	Female (>15 yrs) (married)	Total housing units	Owner occupied housing units	
Alameda	1,443,741	42,842	20,129	11,483	13,159	6,113	80,674
Contra Costa	948,816	11,683	5,544	2,909	3,573	2,106	73,301
Marin	247,289	1,330	608	368	459	188	64,792
San Mateo	707,161	10,535	4,782	2,899	3,783	1,335	83,621
San Francisco	776,733	5,524	3,045	813	2,329	557	72,018
Santa Clara	1,682,585	66,741	29,635	17,992	22,543	8,376	93,374
Solano	394,542	2,869	1,343	699	739	511	56,713
Sonoma	458,614	1,498	687	442	455	205	60,962
TOTAL	6,659,481	143,022	65,773	37,605	47,040	19,391	

*Data for Napa County not available, since number of Asian Indians < 100
SOURCE: 2000 Decennial Census as shown in *factfinder.census.gov*.

TABLE 1.5 Education Level of Asian Indians in 8* Counties of the San Francisco-Oakland Bay Area

San Francisco Bay Area County	Asian Indians—male and female—holding Bachelor's Degree or higher
Alameda	18,831
Contra Costa	4,297
Marin	723
San Mateo	5,588
San Francisco	2,326
Santa Clara	35,658
Solano	676
Sonoma	453
TOTAL	68,552

*Napa County not included since number of Asian Indians < 100
SOURCE: 2000 Decennial Census as shown in *factfinder.census.gov*.

The dot.com Bust

The import of computer professionals from India has lessened considerably since the crash of the dot.com industry, and the general cooling down of the American economy in 2001, and then again, in 2008. The recovery from the 2008 recession in the US remains weak. H-1B quotas that had been lifted during the dot.com boom to 195,000 people, were lowered down to 115,000 after the financial failure of a huge number of high-tech companies. Many Asian Indian high-tech workers, whose Silicon Valley positions were terminated due to the closure of their company or outsourcing to India, were forced to return to India with their families. A few became consultants to US firms but they had no fixed income or position. Some, who had been given pink slips, set up home-based enterprises in which they took high-tech contracts from American firms, and had the work done in India for a lower price.

Conclusion of Statistical Overview

The 2010 Census showed that there were 2,843,391 Asian Indians living in the US in that year. The American Community Survey conducted by the US Census Bureau in 2005 counted 2,319,222 Asian Indians in the US, and the 2000 Census report showed just 1,678,785 Asian Indians residing in the US that year.

The 2010 Census reported that Asian Indians constituted 0.9 per cent of the total population of the US and that their number had increased by 40.9 per cent since the last Census (2000) was taken. The 2010 Census showed that Indians in the US were the second-largest Asian group and that only the Chinese, population of 3.3 million in the US outnumbered Indians in the Asian American group that year. The 2010 Census, also showed that nationwide, Asian Indians constituted 19.17 per cent of the Asian American population and at 14.6 million people, constituted 4.8 per cent of the total population of the US.

The 2010 Census report informed us that though currently relatively small, numbering at just 14,674,252 individuals, the Asian American population in America is the fastest growing racial category in the US and has grown by 43.3 per cent since 2000 (the population of Hispanics and Latinos is also increasing at a very fast pace; please refer to Table 1.1).

The 2000 Census reported that California, New York, and New Jersey are three states with relatively large Asian Indian populations. There are 528,176 Asian Indians in California, constituting 1.4 per cent of the state's total population. Indians currently make up 10.9 per cent of the total Asian American population of California (Census Documents *www.census.gov*).

TABLE 1.6 Race Divisions in the State of California

Race	Percentage of the total population of the State of California, 37.3 million
White, not Hispanic	40.1
Black or African, not Hispanic	5.8
Indian American or Alaskan Native, not Hispanic	0.4
Asian, not Hispanic (Asian Indian)	12.8 (1.4)
Native Hawaiian or some other Pacific Islander, not Hispanic	0.3
Some other race, not Hispanic	0.2
Two or more races, not Hispanic	2.6
Hispanic or Latino (of any race)	37.6
Minority Population	59.9

SOURCE: Census 2010 Documents as shown in *www.census.gov*.

TABLE 1.7 Change in California's Racial Composition in the Last Decade

Race	Change (%)
White	− 5.4
Hispanic	+ 27.8
Asian	+ 30.9
Black	− 0.8
Indian American or Alaskan Native	− 9.3
Native Hawaiian and other Pacific Islander	+ 23.9

SOURCE: Census 2010 Documents as shown in *www.census.gov*.

According to the Census of 2010, California is the most racially diverse state in the nation and there is no particular racial or ethnic category that makes up more than half of the population of California. The 2010 Census counted 4.4 million Asian Americans in California, constituting almost 13 per cent of the total population of California.

FROM LUMBERMAN TO SOFTWARE ENGINEER:
CONTINUITY VERSUS CHANGE

In the early 1900s, the majority of immigrants journeying to the US and Canada were working class Punjabi peasants who came to North America to work as lumbermen, railroad construction workers, and farmhands. Though American legislation put a stop to all Asian migration in the intervening decades, by the mid-1960s, the US again opened its doors to migration from India and other Asian countries. This time however, all immigration quotas were reserved for professionally qualified workers and students. Only technically certified professionals such as doctors, engineers, and academicians were allowed to immigrate to the US. The post-1960s immigration policy of the US did not make any allowances for blue-collar immigration from Asia.

Illegal migration of unskilled labourers has continued unabatedly in the last few decades and despite starting their journey from thousands of miles away, some illegal immigrants from India do make it to the US. Illegal entry is the principal immigration channel of working class men and women from India. Equally, some Indians who end up working in blue-collar occupations in the US obtain entry to the nation by acquiring Green Cards through their professionally qualified siblings, spouses, or adult children who entered the US on the strength of their technical skills, and then become US citizens. In spite of these two sources of Indian working class, the majority of Indian immigrants are highly skilled and educated individuals. The occupational character of the bulk of the post-1960s immigrants from India is white-collar rather than blue-collar.

Amitava Kumar writes: 'The terms of exchange called international migration require scrutiny and even stringent critique. Because to begin with, often the commodities are people, and they are part of an unequal and unjust exchange' (2000: 223). This study argues that in spite of the change in occupational category of the majority of Indian immigrants from labourers to doctors, engineers, academicians, and graduate students, what Kumar calls the 'terms of exchange' have not changed by any significant degree. In the 1900s, Punjabi labourers immigrated to North America because there was no work for them in India. They could stay on in the US and Canada because they agreed to work for longer hours, under worse conditions, and for lower pay than native-born American lumbermen, railroad construction crew, and fruit pickers. There are striking similarities in the current situation of professionally skilled Indian immigrants. Indian engineers, doctors, and Ph.D. holders immigrate to the US because they cannot find suitable work in India. Often, corruption and nepotism choke the few existing avenues of employment in India and the predominantly statist economy fails to provide enough jobs for the millions of technically qualified graduates being churned out by the Indian educational system every year. Therefore, migration out of India is a natural choice for ambitious Indian youths and once they reach American shores, Indian professionals manage to stay on in the US because they are prepared to work longer hours, under worse conditions, and for lesser remuneration than native-born American professionals with similar qualifications. Generally, H-1B visa holders are not choosy about their terms of employment and will take any terms offered to them by their American employers, for they know that they cannot stay on in the US unless an American firm employs them. If his or her employment in the US is terminated, then the H-1B worker must leave the US in less than 30 days. As such, Indian immigrant professionals not only work longer hours, and for less compensation and benefits than their American counterparts, but they also accept employment positions that native-born Americans with comparable skills are unwilling to consider. For example, most Indian software engineers work long hours on complicated projects that must be completed at short notice; innumerable Indian immigrant doctors work in rural areas and inner cities in dangerous conditions; countless Indian immigrant Ph.D. holders teach in tiny community colleges and agricultural universities. These are certainly not the best jobs in their fields and Indian immigrants are certainly not lacking in ability, yet still they feel they have to accept poor positions.

Amitava Kumar has labelled the terms of employment of Indian professionals in the US as 'unjust' or 'unequal'. This study is not quite so extreme in outlook for one cannot ignore the realities of developing world origins and developed world comforts. Even though they often accept positions and salaries rejected by their American counterparts, Indian immigrants often still perceive their current situation in the US to be better than what it would have been had they remained in India. Otherwise, they would surely leave the US and return to India. Supply and demand, relative standards of luxury and hardship, and the will to do better than one's compatriots all drive professional Indian immigrants of the post-1960s era just as much as they previously motivated the Punjabi labourer immigrants of the early 1900s.

FIELDWORK

Due to a combination of the economic boom of the late 1990s and the burgeoning of the high-tech sector in the San Francisco-Oakland Bay Area, a large number of satellite cities grew in the East and South Bay. Technology has acted as a magnet to draw qualified personnel from various parts of the world, particularly South Asia. There was an increase in the H-1B visa programme. In 2000, the US Congress increased the inflow of qualified Indian computer and other professionals into the Silicon Valley. According to figures from the State Department, the number of H-1B visas issued to those from India jumped from 2,697 in 1990 to 15,228 in 1995, and to 55,047 in 2000. After the dot.com bust, the visa quota was brought down to 115,000 again by the Congress. Nevertheless, the Silicon Valley still houses the highest concentration of Indians (and Asians in general), within the Bay Area.

Some successes within the Indian immigrant population are well known, such as Vinod Khosla, co-founder of Sun Microsystems, and Sabeer Bhatia, who founded Hotmail and sold it to Microsoft for $400 million. In the Silicon Valley, Indian venture capitalists such as Kanwal Rekhi are widely revered by the local Indian community for mentoring numerous successful start-up venture founders.

Most Indian families live in Fremont (East Bay) and Cupertino (South Bay). The burgeoning Indian population in the Bay Area (143,022 Indians in 2000, according to the 2000 Census) patronized a growing number of flourishing Indian stores and services there. For example, Naaz 8 Cinema, a small South Asian movie theatre, moved out of its cramped premises in Fremont, into a brand new multiplex movie theatre where eight different new movies from Bollywood are simultaneously shown daily on eight separate screens. There is a similar Indian movie multiplex in Santa Clara, IMC 6, and also innumerable Indian stores in the Bay Area which cater to Indian expatriates. These shops sell Indian groceries, magazines, saris, salwar kameezes, Hindu puja material and some stores specialize in selling Indian gold and diamond jewellery. Almost every neighbourhood in this region has its own Indian, Pakistani, or Bangladeshi restaurant.

The Indians in the Bay Area have also built a community centre in Milpitas where Indian music, dance, and yoga classes are held. The famous Ali Akbar School of Indian Music is also in the Bay Area, as well as numerous other performers and instructors of the Indian arts. There are numerous music, dance, theatre, and movie celebrities who fly in from India and organize shows and lecture-demonstrations in the Bay Area regularly. At least a dozen shows of different Indian cultural genres are held in the Bay Area every week.

There are Sikh gurdwaras and Sikh academies in El Sobrante, San Francisco, Fremont, San Jose, Sunnyvale, Palo Alto, Fairfield, and Tracy. The Stockton gurdwara has been in operation since 1946. There are Indian-Christian churches in San Jose (four in that city), Santa Clara, San Carlos, Fremont, and Livermore, the latter is a Syrian Christian church. The Indian Muslim community in the Bay Area favours their own mosques in San Francisco City, San Jose, Santa Clara, Fremont, Oakland, Hayward, Fairfield, and Vallejo. There is a Jain temple and cultural centre in San Jose. There is also a big Hindu temple in Livermore in the East Bay Area, boasting traditional south Indian temple architecture. There are also several temples in Sunnyvale, Fremont, San Jose, and Concord, where most Indian expatriates in the San Francisco Bay Area live. There is also a Vedanta Society and an ISKCON centre in the Bay Area.

Every major Indian regional community, including Tamil, Telugu, Kannada, Malyali, Bengali, and Maharashtrian, has its own association in the Bay Area. These associations organize regional festivals such as Pongal, Onam, Durga Puja, Navaratri, and Ganesh Chaturthi. Diwali is the occasion for numerous open-air fairs with booths selling traditional Indian food and merchandise, live music and dance from the different states of India and fireworks' display in Paramount's Great America Park in Santa Clara. Indian regional associations and the various Hindu temples in the Bay Area also organize their own Diwali celebrations.

METHODOLOGY AND PERCEPTIONS

Through conducting 60 detailed interviews, I have studied identity issues, immigrant experience, participation in the American workforce, and presence in the Indian immigrant family of professional Indian women in the San Francisco Bay Area. Of these, 40 interviews were with professional Indian immigrant working women in the San Francisco Bay Area, 10 were with non-working Indian immigrant women in the San Francisco Bay Area, and the rest were with professional working women resident in India. All the women interviewed were in professional or semi-professional white-collar occupations at the time the interviews were carried out.

In India, my sample of interviewees expanded as each subject introduced me to other subjects. In America, I conducted fieldwork by immersing myself in the Indian immigrant community in the Bay Area, making contact with professional women at informal parties in Indian immigrant homes. Sometimes a friend would introduce me to her working friends, and at other times I would myself seek out professional career women whom I had heard of from Indian friends. I conducted semi-structured interviews with these women at their home or place of work, or at my own home. The interviews followed the flow of conversation, but I also had a set of questions prepared and so I ensured that the questions were covered at some point in each of the interviews. The interviews were conducted in English, Hindi, Urdu, and Bengali. There were some recurring coded words, such as 'American' for 'Caucasian'. Please note that I have used pseudonyms when referring to my subjects and their locations for though the Indian community in the Bay Area is not small, it is close-knit, and so I feel it would be wise to protect the actual identities of my interviewees and indeed always reassured my subjects that I would disguise their actual identities before the interview.

It occurred to me that these women had dual identities, one for home and the Indian immigrant community, and another for work and their American co-workers. The contrast between the projection of a persona of an English-speaking, Western-attired, aggressive career-oriented professional woman with that of the persona of a Bengali, or Hindi, or Tamil, or Gujarati speaking sari-clad Indian immigrant wife and mother is quite remarkable. The clash between the performance of Western/American cultural practices, and that of Asian/Indian cultural practices provides a stark comparison.

My fieldwork did however reveal that the contrast cannot be presented in such a simple way, for the situation is complicated by various factors such as tenure of residence in the US, occupation, duration of employment, class position before immigrating to the US, marital situation, age, and number of children.

CHAPTER II

⇁⇀

In Search of Success in the American Workplace

INTRODUCTION

THERE HAS BEEN an unabated increase in American women's employment in the past century. The United States Census in 2000 reported that 58.90 per cent of American women over the age of sixteen are employed and that at that time 45 per cent of Asian Indian women in the US work outside the home in paid employment (US 2000 Census Bureau Documents). On the whole, the percentage of Asian Indian women in paid employment in the San Francisco-Oakland Bay Area is the same as the national average, simply because so many female workers from India have been employed in the Silicon Valley and in local biotech firms. Nationally, the majority of first generation Indian immigrant women are educated at least up to high school level and many are also college-educated and proficient in English. A growing number of new female immigrants from India are qualified professionals in their own right, mostly as computer programmers, research scientists, doctors, dentists, or teachers. The percentage of professionally qualified Indian immigrants is higher in the Bay Area than in other parts of the US. However, there is a significant number of Indian immigrant women in semi-professional, service, or blue-collar positions; they work as children's daycare centre employees, babysitters, administrative assistants, secretaries, receptionists, caterers, cooks, shop clerks, hotel employees, cleaning women, tailors, and factory workers. Many also work in family-owned stores, gas stations, and motels.

MOTIVATIONS FOR WORK

Economic Motivation

One of my subjects said, 'Ghar se nikli hoon, to paise kama ke laungi' (Now that I have stepped out of my home, I will bring in some money), and most of my other subjects echoed her sentiments in different words. In my view, the desire to earn money is the principal motivation for Indian immigrant women to go to work. In general, all women in present-day America are more active in the workforce than in previous generations. Paula England argues that the increase in the percentage of working women in the US in recent decades is not only due to the growth in the number of single women in the US, but also due to unprecedented growth in the service sector, a portion of the economy that traditionally employs women. This is useful for the Indian community in the US in that many Indian immigrant women find work in service jobs such as retail sales, financial and accounting operations, medical assistance, computer technical support, contract research, childcare, real estate sales, schoolteaching, and food catering.

Moreover, England also states that recurrent recessions and recoveries in the American labour market in the last two decades have caused great fluctuations in the earning capacity of the American male. This has resulted in a perceived need for wives to have a regular income and the wife's income is deemed to be imperative for the well-being of the family. The wife's earnings are supposed to act as a buffer against possible unemployment or underemployment of the husband. This is certainly true in the Indian community in the Bay Area. One interviewee named Umesh says,

> Nutan's [his wife's] income is essential. We have to pay the house mortgage, car payments, etc. You know how volatile the telecommunications industry is right now. Hundreds of people have already been laid off in the company I work for. You never know, you can't take the risk of living on a single income.

As Valerie Oppenheimer (1982) and others have found, those wives who are subjected to economic pressures are more likely to participate in economic activity and to make a contribution to their families' economic security than others. Lacking job security and financial support from the extended family, professional Indian couples have a precarious existence in the new country, hence two incomes are deemed imperative.

England mentions another factor that is responsible for an increase in the number of working women, that is, women usually now work for a few years before childbirth. The family gets used to their income, hence it is difficult for them to give up their jobs during pregnancy and child-rearing. Until a couple of decades ago, women would leave the workforce in their childbearing and child-rearing years but currently, in order to maintain a stable family income, women remain in work through child-rearing as well. The trend of women working for a number of years before childbirth, and remaining in the workforce through child-rearing is definitely true of the Indian immigrant community in the Bay Area. In fact, desis here come up with uniquely Indian methods of childcare while the new mother goes back to work. It is common practice for the new baby's grandparents to come over to the US for six months at a time to care for the child (the maximum stay allowed by the US visitor visa is six months for a single trip). Not only does the typical Indian professional woman go back to being employed within a couple of months of childbirth, she tends to stay at work even when the children are on vacation from school as they grow up. Here too, the Indian extended family and Indian immigrant community is of great assistance. Grandparents come to spend the long summer vacation in the US, so that the children do not have to spend the summer in expensive summer camps while their parents are at work. Sending children to India to spend the summer with their grandparents is also common. Also, Indian immigrant housewives who are not employed make some money by taking care of their working friends' children during school holidays and vacations. Indian meals, language immersion, and diligent homework supervision are provided in such settings.

Yen Le Espiritu has written that Asian American women work to support their families and to add to the economic well-being of the family. This is especially necessary when many Asian men cannot find satisfactory employment in the US. Espiritu has written that:

Due to the [Asian] men's lack of opportunities, women of colour have had to engage in paid labour to make up the income discrepancies . . . most Asian American women, like other women of colour, do not separate paid work and housework. Their work outside the home is an extension of their domestic responsibilities, as all family members—the women, men, and children—pool their resources to ensure economic subsistence or to propel the family up the economic ladder. (1997: 10)

Espiritu has written about both male and female-led immigration using the examples of Filipino sailors and stewards in the American Navy and Filipino nurses in America.

Indian women follow the Filipino work-migration pattern to some extent. While some immigrant wives provide supplementary incomes, many Indian women come to the US in female-first migration patterns as international students in US universities and guest workers in the software industry. A substantial number of nurses from southern India (Kerala) have come to the US as primary immigrants (George 2005). Many regularly remit large amounts of money from the US to their folks in India. India has higher remittances than any other nation. In 2006, the amount was estimated to be US $32 billion, that is, 5 per cent of the India's GDP. There are more (legal) Non-Resident Indians in the US than in any other nation, hence a large portion of the remittances are likely to originate from the US (Kelleher 2006). Since considerable amounts of cash is sent back to India, the immigrant family needs to expand its income in the US, hence the need for a double income.

Visa Status

All first generation Indian immigrants who have entered the country legally and are working with the proper visas, begin their work life in the US on an H-1B visa. This is an extremely precarious existence. If an H-1B visa holder's employment is terminated, then he must leave the country within a couple of months. In such cases, even if the individual succeeds in finding new employment within that short period, his new employers must obtain a new H-1B visa for him. This is virtually impossible in most cases because the H-1B visa quota is usually filled as soon as the year commences, and so most have to return to India in this situation. To avoid such a scenario, married H-1B holders attempt to obtain double employment and two H-1B visas so that even if the husband loses his own position and H-1B status, he can stay on in the US on the strength of his wife's visa until the new H-1B quota is opened in the next year. The hope is that he will have found work by that time, and his new employers will process a new H-1B for him.

Status Accumulation

Indian immigrant working women support their husbands in their attempts to accumulate status. The research for this study suggests that most of the subjects brought in wealth from the market to the home mainly because they saw that they needed it to not only feed, clothe, and house their families, but also to provide their households with the means to produce the cultural capital necessary for improved status. Writing about batik workers and traders in Java, Suzanne Brenner identifies women as the main producers and conservers of wealth in that community. Women also play a key role in 'domesticating' or 'civilizing' money by investing it in the material and social welfare of their families. They convert it into status, prestige, and cultural value in order to improve their family position in the hierarchies of Javanese society (1998). Similarly, Indian immigrant women earn with a view not only to provide a minimum standard of living for their families, but also to assist their families in climbing to a better position in the class hierarchy.

The Indian community in the US wants to be seen as a 'model minority'. Wealth, expressed as ostentatious consumerism, is a tool in the struggle to gain acceptance by the American mainstream. Richard Harvey Brown explains that 'consumerism—the popular ideology of late capitalism—is produced and disseminated in the form of commodified culture' (2003: 203). 'Advertising creates docile workers who are also desirous consumers dreaming of vacation travel, electronic gadgets, high-powered rifles, and other instruments of identity' (ibid.). Both in the immigrant community in the US, and in India, my subjects were clearly driven by the desire to have many possessions such as brand name clothes, jewellery, furniture, electronic kitchen appliances, cars, real estate, vacations not only within India but also in various famous vacation-destinations all over the world. Rather than performance in work and familial roles, the level and style of consumption is the master manipulator of identity. In the global capitalist era, people project images of themselves mainly through consumption. Of course, consumerism in the US, even among typically thrifty first generation Indians is unsurprising, but the extent to which there is a desire for high-end consumer products among the Indian middle class subjects of this study is a revelation. Whether such consumerism is liberating, and whether it is an advance over patriarchy and feudal class subjectivities are interesting questions to raise. In some sense, it can be argued that consumerism is a progressive force, because it delivers a degree of autonomy. The physical comfort and psychological self-confidence of the subjects is higher than that of their mothers and grandmothers because they dare to step out of the home in order to earn enough to buy, for example, that woollen jacket, or that Cuisinart Food Processor they saw advertised. They have a regular income, a car, a bank account, some money saved up for a rainy day, and a bit of property. It can be argued that hand-in-hand with capitalism and consumerism comes gender equity and familial democracy, which actually enable the hardworking to climb up the class ladder and determine the course of their own lives. For some, it may be a choice to be governed by global corporate bosses and consumerist desires, but for others, their destiny may bind them to suffer enslavement by feudal landlords, patriarchal family elders, and the compulsion to produce maximum offspring to till the crop fields.

Besides status acquired through economic success, status is also achieved through educational and occupational success. Indian immigrants come to the US to acquire educational and occupational prestige. US universities are renowned all over the world, and US corporations are much envied sites of employment. Despite apprehension about hitting the glass ceiling, my subjects reported that employment produced feelings of professional self-worth and skilled effectiveness.

The Expectation to Make Use of Education and Training

Since Indian immigrant women are highly educated, there is an expectation that they should work outside the home in paid positions. Vilma Ortiz found that 71 per cent of Indian immigrant women in the US are educated through high school, and 35 per cent have graduated from college. While 53 per cent of these women are in the labour force, 33 per cent of Indian immigrant women in America are in professional occupations (1994). The 2000 Census also showed that 33 per cent of male Indian immigrants in the US were in professional occupations at that time (US Census Documents Bureau). An analysis of data from the 1980 Census by Xenos, Barringer, and Levin showed that the ratio of female to male income earners among South Asians in the US was 45 per cent (1989: 82). In an older survey conducted in 1977–8 in the New York Metropolitan Area, Leonard-Spark and Saran found that 40 per cent of the married female Asian Indian immigrant respondents worked full-time, 10 per cent worked occasionally, and 7 per cent worked part-time (1980: 153).

Haya Steir also found the high level of education among Indian women in the US remarkable. They have 14.5 years of schooling on average and this makes it more likely that they will seek and secure employment. A woman's decision to enter the labour force is affected not only by economic factors, but also by their family context. Some women work because their families need their economic contribution, others work in response to expected productivity in the labour market (1991).

Women who have been devoted to excelling in their studies and career all their lives find that their career remains an important component of their self-image, and an essential bolster for self-esteem, even after marriage and motherhood. This pushes them out of their home and into the labour market. Products of modern middle class and elite Indian nuclear families of the 1960s and 1970s, in families in which two children are the norm, and where the parents put most of their energies into training their sons and daughters to become brilliant doctors, engineers, or scientists, cannot imagine a life exclusively devoted to cooking, cleaning, and child-rearing. They have been trained to work in professional employment outside the home, and they feel that their lives are balanced and complete only if they have a successful career. Their mothers and grandmothers may have only been educated so that they could obtain a good marriage, but present-day women have been educated so that they can build careers for themselves. Most middle class families in India favour sons over daughters, but in many families, especially those families where there are no sons (and there are many such families, for in this class, few couples have more than two, or at the most, three children), daughters become the bearers of the ambitions of their parents.

Marriage does not drastically reduce their drive to work. In keeping with their demographic propensity for marriage, 71 per cent of Indian women in the US are married, yet 53 per cent of them are employed (Ortiz 1994). Marital status plays a key role in deciding employment status. Married women are less likely to work than single women. Most of the Indian women who immigrated to the US in the 1960s and 1970s came as wives of male primary immigrants. In the last two decades, Indian wives have continued to come in large numbers, but they come with professional and technical qualifications that can be easily transferred to the US job market, hence they easily find employment here. Also, in the last two decades, quite a few unmarried Indian women have come as international students to American universities and stayed on and found work. A few Indian women have been directly recruited from India to work in the American computer software industry or in postdoctoral research in American universities. Some of the women have married men who they met after they came to the US as primary immigrants, but they tend to continue to work after marriage.

The Desire for Agency within the Immigrant Family

Many Indian immigrant women I have spoken to said that they work so that they have a say within their family so agency is an important motivation for work. Asian American women work because they want to contribute to the family income, but another important motivation is that work brings empowerment. Many of my interviewees said they could not imagine giving up their jobs, since failure to bring in an income would diminish their authority within the family. For example, Rajmani said:

I work hard all day. I do whatever I want to, I don't have to ask my husband's or my parents' permission for anything, though of course, I always discuss with them. I work hard so that my family can live a good life. That is why my daughter says, 'Mommy, you're the boss in this family!'

In a related but separate issue, my interviewees said that they are happy to have an income of their own so that they can spend money to strengthen ties to their natal families and friends without being questioned by their husbands. This is revolutionary in the Indian context for it transforms the daughter's role from 'burden' to 'producer'. Traditionally the wife's relatives are expected to only provide services and gifts, but in the new equation, they are allowed to be at the receiving end of gifts and services from a wage-earning daughter even after her marriage. Writing about Keralite nurses, Sheba Mariam George has elucidated the principle of 'connective autonomy'. According to this theory, while the nurses gain social and economic mobility and independence through paid employment, they enjoy these advantages mainly within natal family relationships and female friendship obligations. In giving equal, if not more, importance to their natal families and personal friends even after marriage, they democratize the traditionally patriarchic chauvinistic norms of the typical Keralite family, and question assumed rights of husbands and husbands' families over wives (2005).

It is possible to suggest economic motivations to be the primary cause for seeking employment within my subject group. The ambition for upward class mobility drove the majority of my interviewees for they wanted to be a part of the American dream, part of the American middle class. Also, proliferating consumerism compelled the subjects to increase their cash flows and credit allowances. The significant educational qualifications of my subject group did not automatically ensure employment, but they were of great assistance in the job search. Equally, concerns about visa status drove many of my interviewees to work. It is important to mention however that employment brought increased agency to women, and therefore once they obtained employment, none of the women interviewed for this study wanted to give it up.

SOCIAL INTERACTIONS IN THE WORKPLACE

Some occupations require more social interaction with colleagues and clients than others. For example, a physician, a university professor, or a financial consultant has to constantly interact with patients, students, and clients respectively. In contrast, a computer software engineer or research scientist spends most of their time engaged in solitary occupations such as writing code or conducting experiments, they barely have to interact with their co-workers or clients.

Dr Urmila Bagchi is a physician who has lived in the US for more than two decades. She says that she is very comfortable in her interactions with her patients and does not feel that she is disadvantaged by her colour or ethnicity. She explains that she does not attempt to project herself differently at work nor does she try to put on an American accent for the benefit of her patients.

Megha is an assistant professor at a Northern Californian university. She usually teaches two courses every semester and naturally, a major portion of her time is spent in interaction with her students. She says:

I present myself to my students as a teacher and then, when it is relevant, I'll say, well from my experience of India, I'll introduce my experience of India, or I'll . . . say something about America that makes it clear that I am an outsider. Or sometimes, when talking about America, I would say something like 'But this is a problem *we* have to face', in the sense I am saying we as an American. So I do both, and I'm not entirely sure that it is conscious.

Shupriya has been an information technology manager at Stanford University for the last two years. Before that, she worked for five years as an auditing and information systems consultant at Schourers. Her work is such that it involves constant interaction with the people whose auditing and information systems she is in charge of: 'In my job, it's mainly to go out and meet people and see what their systems do, try to find out about their systems, their applications, in a very short time, and come to some sort of a conclusion, and maybe help them to do their work better'. She says that she is very comfortable interacting with all the non-Indians she encounters on the job: 'When I had a consulting job, it was mostly, especially back East, probably 95 per cent non-Indians. But in the Valley of course it is different.'

Aparajita is a human resources manager at a start-up computer software company in the Silicon Valley. She used to work in a similar position in a Bay Area department store for a couple of years before she joined her present employer. She is in her mid-30s and has been in the US for five years. Her job is all about managing people but she admits that she finds her work rather challenging, 'I don't think people who work with technology . . . interact with people as much as I do. My job is to work with people. Sometimes, due to the cultural gap, I do face some problems.'

Though her previous place of work was a huge department store with innumerable branches on the West Coast, she now works in a relatively small company that is owned and run by Indian immigrants.

Since my study is about Indian professional women in the San Francisco-Oakland Bay Area, more than half of the women I observed and interviewed were computer programmers and testers in the Silicon Valley. With the exception of group meetings, their work involved little interaction with colleagues or clients. For example, Mrigakshi, a software tester at Sabine Information Solutions, spends her entire day testing various software applications on her computer. She rarely leaves her desk and does not even venture to the office cafeteria most days. There are very few Indians in her office, and she said of her colleagues, 'I wouldn't say that they are very great friends. But I feel very comfortable with them. And I feel they too are very comfortable'. Mrigakshi says she has trouble relating to American women because they are too independent. For example, they speak of divorce lightly, not understanding that even discussing such a calamity is a taboo for most traditional Indian women.

Nila, a postdoctoral researcher in a social science department in a university in Northern California, spends most of her days working alone in her office at the university. She does not teach and she interacts with other people at the department only during departmental meetings or at the occasional lunch date or coffee break with some of her colleagues. She is however glad that she has a reason to get out of her house, an office to work in, library facilities, and a chance of getting her research published, but she does not have much else at work.

Navneet is a computer software developer who also spends most of her day on her own. In her words, 'There is not much interaction with others at work', except at weekly meetings.

Romila is a postdoctoral researcher in the genetic engineering department of another well-known university in the Bay Area. She spends the whole day at the laboratory, returning home as late as 2 a.m. most nights, but she rarely has much social interaction with her colleagues, speaking to them only regarding her professional needs. Her supervisor was going to send her back to India once her contract was over, but she managed to get a grant from National Institutes of Health (NIH). Now she has to work in two separate laboratories to do the work she has received funding for because some essential equipment is in the second laboratory, which she can only access after the regular researchers there have finished their day's work. She says that she is glad that there is no need for social contact with her colleagues because she cannot understand them. For one thing, she seldom sees the humour in their jokes: 'I laugh, but inside I am thinking, "So what was the point of that joke?"'

When Indian women come to the US, they realize that the formal gender relations expected of 'decent' women and men in India are considered strange in America. Indian women learn to be friendly in their behaviour with men in America since that is the expectation. To show how different America is from India, Niharika says this about gender relations in the Indian workspace:

When I was a hardware engineer in the Calcutta Municipal Corporation, I was the only female engineer there; until I told them that I was an engineer, most people took it for granted that I was the receptionist. Anyway, I had to dress very formally so that people there would respect me and take me seriously. I only wore saris, never salwar kameez, and, of course, I could not dream of going to work in casual or Western clothes. I had to be very careful that I was not too friendly with my male colleagues, because otherwise they would think I was 'cheap' or 'forward', and take advantage of me.

Indian women hesitate to appear to be too friendly with Indian men, but Indian cultural standards are irrelevant during social contact with American men. In fact, in the US it is considered rude to be 'cold' or 'distant', even in casual social exchanges, hence Indian women are friendlier while interacting with American men.

JOB RETENTION AND ADVANCEMENT

Data entry and data processing jobs have already moved offshore, and other computer-based areas such as software design, computer graphics, data-based research, animated video production services, and computer aided design (CAD) are performed mostly by H-1B visa status foreign immigrants. These immigrant workers are often paid lower wages than those demanded by equally proficient native-born American techies. Also, electronic surveillance of workers has made it possible for managers to closely observe their employees without face-to-face contact. Given the current devaluation of technical and service positions in the San Francisco Bay Area, it is important to address the issue of whether women workers are in a worse position when compared to their male counterparts.

Gender barriers to advancement at work were discussed in the interviews conducted for this research. Aparajita mentioned gender-based problems with her supervisory work at LM, a big department store:

I have faced gender discrimination in LM here, and in *deshe* [India] too, because some men have problems accepting a woman as a supervisor. I have seen that there are many [men] who have a problem accepting us. This is so in both nations, even in India I faced problems.

Moving on to a separate type of gender discrimination, sex segregation of jobs continues to be a prominent reality of the American labour force. Most women work in occupations in which most employees are female; and most men work in occupations which are filled mostly by men. Approximately 60 per cent of men or women would have to change occupations in order to integrate all occupations in the American labour force (England 1992: 12). Assembly line workers in the electronic industry, clerks in retail stores, secretaries, schoolteachers, nurses, and librarians are mostly women (Ibid.: 14). Full integration would mean a situation in which the ratio of men to women in the various occupations would be the same as the ratio of men to women in the labour force as a whole (this was slightly over 40 per cent in 1980). I mostly interviewed female Indian immigrant computer industry professionals, academicians, physicians, and research scientists. These women had largely escaped occupational gender segregation, that is, they were not in occupations traditionally filled only or mostly by women. However, I also interviewed many Indian immigrant women who were employed in children's preschools and daycare institutions. Like computer software writing, preschool teaching is also a very popular occupation among Indian immigrant women. Preschool teachers are almost all women, which is perhaps a reason why they are paid so little as a group. Ayesha, in charge of two-year-olds in a South Bay private school says, 'I work full-time, yet my pay is so low, [and] it barely covers the subsidized school fees of my two daughters who are studying in the same school I teach in.' Rajmani, also a teacher in a local preschool, complains 'I have been working in the same place for more than six years now, yet I still earn peanuts, it is so frustrating!' However, Indian immigrant preschool teachers did not report getting paid less than their American counterparts as all preschool teachers are paid very little.

Turning to the question of race, this study will now address the ways in which the subjects encountered the issue of race. Initially, Aparajita stated that she had never faced any problems regarding race relations. Aparajita said:

I have never faced any discrimination, even when I was studying, even when I used to work before, even here, nowhere have I faced any discrimination. A place like LM [a department store chain] where there are so many problems, there they accepted me very well. But in LM, because I was promoted very fast, people didn't like that. That is why they weren't accepting my supervisory authority at first. But that's a different reason, not related to race.

However, later in the interview, Aparajita admitted that she was daunted by the absence of racial and ethnic minorities in her department, 'There are few Indians working in Human Resources, and so I feel a bit out of place.'

Mrigakshi is a software tester, which is an entry level position. She says that:

[As a non-White], when you are really getting very high level then at some point of time maybe you will not be allowed to rise any higher . . . When it comes to being the vice president of research of the company, definitely they have biased opinion; Very few non-White people have really gone to the top. I think that is very sad.

Very few of the Indian immigrant professional women I spoke to in the Bay Area had experienced any racism, but what they had experienced was social unease. Some of my interviewees did mention some level of social exclusion at work. For example, Rani related how she was often excluded from after-work social events organized by her colleagues. In many ways, this can be seen as only natural, for people tend to naturally gravitate to social others who are as much like themselves as is possible. In the absence of others who are 'like them' (of similar ethnic and cultural heritage), Indian immigrant professional women naturally find themselves without social 'sisters' (or social groups) in their workplace, and consequently, with fewer social mentors or followers than mainstream Americans. Also, most of my informants were married, with or without children, and hence they were mostly occupied with family-events after work. Commitment to family-centred activities in the evenings and weekends did not leave much time for socializing with American colleagues, many of whom were single.

Whether or not the perception of a tendency towards social exclusion was justified, none of my interviewees complained of any discrimination as far as their work was concerned. In fact, many of my interviewees emphasized that they had never been held back in their professional career on account of their race. This may be because they work in occupations that are relatively open to non-Whites. Shalini, a Director of Product Development and Financial Applications at Delphi Technology said that she had been 'lucky' in that she had never experienced her race or gender as barriers to her rise to middle management:

I have had a very positive experience in my work throughout. It has been truly merit-based. I have been able to rise through the ranks to my present position of Director. My ethnicity and gender have not been a bottleneck for me. I have always had very understanding managers.

Rani is a postdoctoral fellow in a science department in a university in the Bay Area. Having gone to graduate school in the US, she has been there since the late 1980s. Rani is grateful to be in academia for in that field, people are open-minded and culturally enlightened, 'I did not feel any outright discrimination at any point. I think being in an academic environment was why I didn't face any discrimination.'

Urmila, an Indian immigrant physician reported that far from facing any discrimination at work because of her ethnicity, it has been somewhat of an advantage because, at least in the Bay Area, Indian physicians are well reputed.

Namita, a Development Manager at Delphi Technology, said that far from being discriminated against, Indians are preferred for technical positions in the computer industry in the Silicon Valley because of their well known information technology skills:

In fact Indians get higher preference than others. They are looked upon as hard working, and their quality of work is very high. . . . Of course, there are some departments such as sales and marketing where there are no foreign people—Indians are much more technical. I think Indians do very well if they realize their limitations and stick to technical stuff.

In general, Indian immigrant women may face problems of incorporation due to lack of social inclusion at work. Despite such structural difficulties however, they derive immense satisfaction from the contributions they make to their workplace, and the professional appreciation they receive there.

In conclusion, some Indian immigrant professional working women do face gender discrimination in the US, but, having undergone similar instances of male chauvinism in India, they are habituated to it. Most of my respondents were in gender-integrated professions, but those women who were in gender-segregated occupations such as preschool teaching had to accept low wages and minimal benefits. None of my respondents reported racial discrimination at work. In fact some said that workers of Indian ethnicity are at a professional advantage in occupations such as software writing, technical support, and medicine. Many of my subjects did mention lack of social inclusiveness at work. Failure to penetrate social cliques at work might hinder career development to some extent, but my subjects were not really bothered by it since they derived professional satisfaction from their work, and had their own ethnic social spheres outside of work.

THE RISK OF IMMIGRANT STATUS

Indian immigrant workers are disadvantaged by their dependency on H-1B visas. Many Asian immigrant workers lack a Green Card or citizenship, so all they have is the H-1B work permit visa that allows employment in the US for three years. It can be renewed only once for three more years, after which they must obtain a Green Card or leave the US. Such workers tend to lack the economic resources and social-support networks that could sustain them for even a short time in case of termination of employment. In fact, their very disadvantage has given an advantage to immigrant workers in that American employers are eager to hire docile, technically-trained, English speaking Indian workers who do not demand high wages. This has led to the creation of 'ghettoes' of Indian tech workers in certain American companies in the Bay Area. However, when company profits become slim and the corporation is forced to let go of some of its employees, then Indian techies are just as likely as native-born Americans to be handed pink slips to terminate their employment.

The Failure of the Dot.Com Industry and the Economic Slowdown

In the 1960s, 1970s, and 1980s, many Indian immigrants came to the US as international students and as employees of American corporations and universities (as mentioned in Chapter I). However, in the 1990s, a new wave of information systems engineers arrived to the point that approximately 115,000 immigrant high-tech workers poured into the US annually, most of them from India and China. There was such high demand for foreign-trained, high-tech workers because American tech companies faced an immense shortage of qualified workers in the US, and they claimed that they could do with more from outside the nation. H-1B workers themselves said that they were in demand because they were very good at their job even though such workers remain at the mercy of their employers until they obtain a Green Card, and may have to accept slightly smaller salaries and lesser benefits than their native-born colleagues.

It is widely acknowledged that directly employed H-1B workers are more secure than H-1B contractual workers. Contractual workers are temporary employees of staffing agencies that import foreign workers, mostly computer programmers from India, and then contract them to work for high-technology and other firms in the Silicon Valley. Staffing agencies or 'body shops' flourished in the high-tech boom of the late 1990s. These staffing agencies charged high hourly rates for the workers services: $100 per hour was the going rate before the dot.com crash. High hourly rates enabled staffing agencies to recoup the costs of importing the workers for import costs were usually a couple of thousand dollars per worker. However, the workers were paid only a fraction of what the agency charged for their services, since the agency pocketed a large percentage as commission. Many Indians in the Bay Area ran such 'body shops' before the high-tech industry crashed.

Staffing services routinely imported more workers than they had projects in hand for. In some cases, benched contractual workers were not paid any salary at all, and were given only a meagre allowance to tide them over until the agency found a suitable project for them. 'Body shops' held their workers with the threat that they would ship them back to their home country if they complained. The Department of Labour has recorded cases where 'body shops' charged workers a fee of $10,000–$25,000 if they left before their contract was up. Investigations by the Labour Department in the latter half of the 1990s revealed more than two million dollars owed in back wages to H-1B visa holders (*San Francisco Chronicle*, 5 October 2000). However, as they were under the constant threat of deportation if their employers were to withdraw their visa sponsorship, most H-1B workers failed to report such abuses by their employers.

US employers lobbied for increasing numbers of H-1B workers during the high-tech industry boom. Notwithstanding the high influx of H-1B workers into America, tech companies threatened to relocate their research and development facilities overseas unless the Congress increased the quota of H-1B visas. President Clinton also supported the lifting of H-1B quotas. Given the factors described above, it was almost inevitable that in October 2000, both the Senate and the House of the US Congress overwhelmingly approved a bill that nearly doubled the number of temporary visas for skilled high-tech workers. The bill raised the annual quota of H-1B visas for workers holding bachelor's degrees from 115,000 to 195,000 for the duration of the next three years. The immigration legislation of 2,000 mainly benefited prospective entrants from India and China, the principal suppliers of H-1B workers.

Just as the Silicon Valley was the epicentre of the digital boom of the 1990s, the Silicon Valley was also the epicentre of the dot.com crash of 2001. Nationwide, some 300,000 high-tech jobs were terminated in 2001 alone, many of which were located in the Silicon Valley (*India Currents*, 1 October 2001: 36). Since more than half of the Indians in the Bay Area were computer techies, Indians in the Bay Area were hit hard by both the calamitous failure of dot.coms as well as the massive personnel cutbacks at high-tech companies.

The Silicon Valley is acknowledged to be the point of origin of the high-tech wave that led the economy in the late 1990s. From 1998 to 2000, internet companies and dot.coms rose swiftly to exceptional stock values and unparalleled investor confidence. However, by 2001 they were out of investor favour and were unable to make profits, and so dot.coms quickly fell in value and dozens of them were forced to shut down. By May 2001, nine of the top twenty companies in the San Francisco Bay Area had collectively laid off 40,000 employees. Since the beginning of 2001, the American unemployment rate had been rising steadily; the jobless were numerous in California and particularly in the Bay Area. According to the US Bureau of Labour Statistics, by November 2001, the US unemployment rate rose to 5.7 per cent and in the same month, the California rate rose to a new high of 6 per cent of the population out of work. In San Francisco, 6.1 per cent out of work, and Santa Clara County had 6.6 per cent facing unemployment (*San Francisco Chronicle*, 15 December 2001: B1).

As a result of the economic slowdown of 2001, the demand for H-1B workers was reduced dramatically. In 2000, the largest employers across the nation planned to recruit 1.6 million people into positions that required technical skills. By 2001 however, there was a demand for only 900,000 new technically-qualified workers and the demand for information technology professionals had dropped by 44 per cent in just one year (*India Abroad*, 13 April 2001: 36). In keeping with the trends reported above, in 2001, US employers slowed down their rate of application for H-1B visas just a year after the Congress 2000 legislation that lifted the H-1B quota from 115,000 to 195,000.

It is very probable that the first employment sector to feel the impact of the high-tech industry sector meltdown were the staffing agencies, or 'body shops'. By mid-2001, most consultancy firms had dropped their hourly rates for H-1B or B1 visa holders with web-related skills by 25–50 per cent (*India Abroad*, 13 April 2001: 36). By March 2001, Somnath Ghosh, president of Specsoft, a staffing firm with offices in San Jose and Bangalore, was forced to reduce the hourly rate charged for tech professionals from $100 an hour to $75 per hour. Equally, he used to bring in at least ten new consultants from India every month, but he stopped new hiring altogether.

Recruiting firms also suffered due to the economic downturn in the high-tech sector. In the heyday of the technological industry, headhunters recruited high volumes of tech professionals for large corporations and start-ups, but by 2001, firing rather than hiring became the norm.

By the end of 2001, the number of new H-1B visa workers coming into the high-tech sector had slowed down to a trickle. Of the thousands of H-1B visa holders who came into the country during the Silicon Valley digital boom, like many others during the high-tech industry slump, thousands of Indian H-1B workers received employment termination notices. Murali Krishna Devakaronda of the Immigration Support Network (ISN) said, 'I know plenty of H-1B people who are getting laid off left and right, just like American citizens' (*San Francisco Chronicle,* 21 March 2001). H-1B visa holders cannot stay on in the US once they are laid off but the INS policy is not very clear on how long an H-1B visa holder can stay on in the US after termination of employment. Despite the consequences of employment termination for H-1B workers, employers could not do anything but let go of more and more employees in the US including both immigrant and native-born workers.

Many corporations also began to open offices overseas where the same work carried out in America could be done at a fraction of the cost. Other companies formed business alliances with Indian or Chinese companies and outsourced positions to these new units located in India. In fact, in some instances, employees located in America were told to train their successors who were going to do the same work from offices located in India. The outsourcing of jobs to India led to a backlash against Indians in general, including resentment against those Indians who had worked in American corporations for a many years.

For both native-born Americans in the computer industry and Indians employed in American corporations, 2001 was a traumatic year. Since the tech crash of 2001, most advertisements for jobs state that the employer is not ready to sponsor visa processing and so once an H-1B worker is 'out of status', it is very difficult for them to find work in the US legally.

Besides H-1B visa holders, innumerable Green Card holders and US citizens of Indian origin also lost their jobs in the dot.com bust. They did not face the threat of deportation, but they still struggled to pay rent, house mortgages, health insurance, car payments, and other living costs for themselves and their families. Kasturi, a sales administrator who has a Green Card, says, 'You know we are going through a rough time. My husband lost the job he has had the last ten years. Now it is difficult for him to start looking for work again. You know when something goes wrong, it is the woman who bears the brunt. Things are very difficult at home right now'. Ruchir, another Green Card holder, worked as a manager at Delvica. When the company closed down, he was left with a negligible severance package and valueless Delvica stocks.

It is clear that the corporate culture in the Bay Area had changed drastically in the space of a single year in 2001. Previously, tech professionals were compensated for the average of sixteen hours of work put in each day with corporate sponsored meals provided at the workplace virtually every working day. In 2001, the work hours remained the same, but there was no food catering in the office and bonuses such as corporate sponsored trips or Christmas parties became a thing of the past. The 2000–1 recession even drove down house prices and rental property rates in the Bay Area for the first time in a decade.

PROFESSIONAL WOMEN IN INDIA

In order to examine the origins of Indian immigrant professional working women in America, I also studied their sending community. Thus, I conducted focused interviews with a number of professional working women in India discussing their work, identity, and self. These women included physicians, academicians, high-school teachers, filmmakers, and research scholars. My findings among Indian white-collar working women will now be discussed in order to compare and contrast their attitudes to work and their experiences in the Indian workplace with the motivations and work-experiences of Indian immigrant professional women in American.

Ambivalence about Women's Employment in India

Writing about urban middle or upper class Indian women who are well-educated and who have white-collar jobs, Lebra, Paulson, and Everett comment on their prominence in Indian society. They note that participation of women in the workforce is much higher in rural areas than in urban areas. However, in spite of the pervasiveness of gainful female employment in rural areas and among the urban poor, it is 'women in urban white-collar jobs, professions, and administration' who have 'high visibility'. Lebra, Paulson, and Everett show that 'new employment opportunities in these [white-collar jobs, science-based and technology-oriented professions, and administration] have absorbed women from the middle and upper classes who are educationally qualified' (1984: 288). Mostly resident in urban areas, such women are in a position to demand certain minimum rights for themselves since they have excellent educational and professional qualifications. Occupying high-paying professional or administrative employment positions, such women are able select the most suitable childcare and medical services available, and benefit from the 'freedom which education, training, and economic means provide' (1984: 295). The authors also note that such upper class women have the support of extended family and paid domestic help. Thus, unlike working mothers in the US, upper class working women in India have few problems with housework and childcare despite their absence from home.

Interestingly, Lebra, Paulson, and Everett conclude that in spite of the prominence and the successful careers of highly educated upper class women, and in spite of the indispensability of female income in most Indian families, the core of the Indian woman's identity continues to remain in her familial role: 'The family is the social context within which all Indian women live and work and have their identity' (1984: 293).

In a personal interview, Madhu Kishwar, an activist who founded a feminist organization called 'Manushi', surprised me by agreeing with the conservative Indian ideal described by Lebra, Paulson, and Everett in that she advocated that women should either live in a joint family so that their children are well cared for by their grandparents or aunts while their mothers are at work, or that they should give up the idea of employment outside the home. Kishwar's view is an interesting variation of Lebra, Paulson, and Everett's notion that the Indian public believes that whenever possible, Indian wives and mothers must devote their lives to care of their conjugal and extended family from within the home. Thus for many people, the ideal Indian woman is not a career woman.

The ambivalence of the Indonesian public towards the *karier* (career) women, as described by Suzanne Brenner below, is very similar to Indian attitudes towards professional working women:

The career woman has been made into a larger-than-life symbol of the positive and negative aspects of modernization. *Wanita karier* ambiguously signifies a woman who is admired for her ability to participate in the modern economy, but who is at the same time fundamentally suspect for her presumed selfishness and lack of attention to her family. According to popular portrayals, she may become overly engrossed with her work, causing her to neglect her family's needs. (1998: 242–3)

The question of how to explain the ideological rejection of gainful employment for Indian family women is complex. For centuries, female work in India has not been confined to housekeeping and child-rearing, but has included agriculture and household production in cottage industries. This study thus concludes that the separation of female work/careers from the female role in the home or family is a relatively modern phenomenon.

Writing about Indonesia, Brenner provides some suggestions as to why women's employment currently causes anxiety in nations in which women have customarily worked outside the home in economically productive activities for many centuries. She explains that 'the idea of the "career woman" becomes a problem at precisely the moment when such a category is *recognized* and opposed to another imported category, that of "housewife"' (1998: 243). Thus, following Brenner, I believe that in India too, the idealization of women devoting all their energies to homemaking and mothering, to the exclusion of all other activities is a recent social phenomenon, claiming affiliation to old tradition; its aim is to pose an alternative to the modern idea of career-building as a goal for women to strive for.

Partha Chatterjee has pointed out that the nationalist construction of the ideal upper class Indian woman who embodied the qualities of feminity, spiritualism, modesty, self-sacrifice, benevolence, devotion, religiosity, cultural refinement, and social responsibility was meant to challenge the colonial discourse about the subjugation and oppression of Indian women as such. This ideal was supposed to help women to fulfil their main purpose in life: to nurture their families and maintain their Indian spirit. The nationalist model of the enlightened Indian woman elevated her to the status of the spiritual and cultural sustainer of her household, and it served to lift her above retrograde practices such as sati, purdah, confinement in the women's quarters (*andar-mahal*), and illiteracy, that Indian society had become infamous for during the colonial era. The vast majority of Indians still look upon the nurturing, spiritual, and cultural role of the Indian women as her most important role, yet practicality demands a career and a steady salary to contribute to the joint household income. Numerous male relatives of my informants spoke nostalgically about how most of the women in their own families used to selflessly focus on running the household smoothly and bringing up their children in the best possible manner, they did not concentrate on proving their capabilities in their employment careers as most modern Indian women do.

Motivations for Work among Professional Women in India

The women interviewed for this study always said that they work to 'keep themselves occupied'. However the women themselves admitted that a double income is necessary to cope with India's high rate of inflation. From the women's own testimony, it was also clear that their incomes are actually very necessary to maintain their own, and their families' appetite for the consumption of multinational goods that are now available in the recently liberalized Indian market. The new Indian middle class has been globalized due to this liberalization and also because of multinational corporate job openings in India. The availability of brand name consumer products in India has opened the floodgates to spending on credit. Items earlier thought of as luxuries are now considered necessities, and only double income families tend to be successful in the race to obtain an international standard of life within Indian borders.

In her book on Malaysian factory women, Aihwa Ong writes that a woman's income is said to be 'useful but inessential' in Malaysia. Malaysian factory supervisors say that the typically young women who come to work in the factories usually use their wages on casual purchases. That is, they might contribute to the family income, but they are not the breadwinners. Yet, the fact remains that their salaries can sometimes make the difference between familial economic survival or ruin (1987). There is a similar hypocrisy prevalent in India for female contributions to the household income are usually de-emphasized in Indian families (Standing 1985). However, in modern day India's consumerist market, they can make the difference between a balanced checkbook and bankruptcy.

All the women I interviewed also said that they worked because they wanted to establish an independent identity of their own, one that is separate from daughter, wife, or mother and they wanted respect from their family and from society in general. They wanted to make use of the education they had worked so hard to acquire. Some of the younger women mentioned that their own mothers were working women and so they saw them as role models. Many of the younger women also said that they could not imagine themselves living a life spent entirely at home, for then, in Renita's words, life would be 'a blank'. Many of the women talked of how being employed boosted their status at home and outside. Aarti, a postdoctoral research scholar said that, 'My income gives me importance. Now that a fat amount of money is coming in, my in-laws and husband give me more importance'. She is proud to be a working woman, because 'we working women are going like men to office meetings, making decisions, we get to see the world'. Aarti emphasized that she was proud that she was an officer, not a clerk: 'When I reach my office, I feel I am an officer, all the clerks [mostly males] are my subordinates'. Thus motivations to work for the majority of my Indian subjects were based on a desire for independent identity formation, respect within the family, and status in the outside world. These attitudes do not fit with the conservative dominant ideology that women should devote themselves above all to the home and family, yet these feelings cannot be ignored for they are prevalent among Indian professional working women.

Gender Discrimination in the Workplace

The women who discussed their experiences in the Indian workplace with me were all in professional or semi-professional occupations. Most of the women reported that they did face some overt gender discrimination in the workplace. However, they were thankful that due to their professional status, they were at least protected from rape, sexual molestation, and other types of sexual harassment directed against working women of the labouring class, or even against women in lower-tier white-collar occupations such as that of a secretary, or personal assistant. Renita, a postdoctoral fellow says:

At this level there isn't much gender discrimination, especially in a big city like Delhi. In any case, the academic world is broad-minded, so there is little discrimination . . . but the bureaucratic atmosphere and gender biases at work do push women back.

Aarti, a research officer in a semi-governmental research institute says:

In India, even if a woman is a professional or even if she holds a high-level white-collar job, she still faces some discrimination. Discrimination persists if a man heads the organization; there is less of it if a woman is the head of the institution. One reads of incidents such as a personal assistant being raped or molested by her male boss, it is not that easy to do such things to higher level white-collar employees, but discrimination still exists. For example, women are told that they are not suitable to become the head of the department, the excuse is that they will not be able to manage the department.

Bipasana, a physician says:

Professionally, I never felt any gender discrimination, I topped the MBBS class in my university. . . . At the officer level, professional women in India do not face any problem. At this level, those who are having extra-marital affairs are doing it of their own choice; they are not coerced into it. But sexual harassment does exist at the lower level.

Beena, a physician who teaches in a Medical College, complained that she was not selected in a hospital job when she was pregnant with her second child because the selection panel doubted her ability to perform adequately in her job while pregnant. 'That was a blatant act of discrimination', she commented. However, from the administrative point of view the selection panel were within their rights obviously.

Despite this range of experiences, professional working women in India appear to face more gender discrimination than their contemporaries who have immigrated to the US because anti-discrimination legislation is not as stringently enforced in India as it is in America.

SOCIAL INTERACTION AT WORK

Many of the women I spoke to described an active social life at the workplace; another attraction of working. Bipasana said:

I have made friends with some office colleagues whose outlook is similar to mine. They are from all different parts of India. We chat during working hours. We also chat on the phone after work hours, problem solving is made easier if we discuss our problems with each other. Sometimes a group of us goes off to see a cinema.

Saraswati, a high schoolteacher says, 'I have my own friends from work. We get off work at the same time. We all go from work to have lunch together at a restaurant, or we go to the Dilli Haat or the Surajkund Mela.'

In general, I found deeper social interaction with colleagues among the interviewees living in India than among the subjects resident in the US. This may be because Indians who have left their homeland have a harder time penetrating social cliques in America both at work and outside, than those who stayed behind in India.

CONSERVATISM AT WORK: STANDARDS
OF FEMALE 'DECENCY'

Discussing general societal attitudes to career women (*wanita karier*) in Indonesia, Brenner argues that there is a common fear that 'her independence might lead her into adulterous affairs that could destroy her marriage and family' (1998: 242–3). Due to a similar public hysteria in India about female morality at the workplace, I found that my subjects were extremely cautious about interaction with male colleagues after work. Aparna Mahajan, a senior member of the Rajya Sabha (National Senate) says that she does not socialize with her colleagues outside of work hours mainly because she lives on her own in Delhi:

I don't socialize with my work people usually. Here in the Rajya Sabha [National Senate], it would have been nice to socialize, but my husband doesn't live in Delhi, so he can't attend any of my parties. So I don't ask people to my home. In Delhi, I am a single woman for all intents and purposes, and the respect people have for me would get tarnished if I did invite my colleagues to my home.

However, all of my respondents from India mentioned friendships with other females at work and if they had social connections with male colleagues, they did not mention them. On the other hand, the subjects resident in the US were not hesitant about talking about inter-gender friendships at work.

Summing Up

I have included my observations about the attitudes and experiences of professional working women in India because they are the sending community for my subjects in the US. This work aimed to show what sort of a milieu my America-resident respondents emerged from, and the continuities and changes in their motivations and work habits displayed in their participation in the American labour force.

First, I found that there is a certain ambivalence towards career women in India: the dominant ideology dictates that women should devote themselves to their families, but due to the recent liberalization of the economy, only double income couples are able to keep up with present rates of inflation and consumption. Therefore, Indian women cannot adhere to the dominant ideal of confinement at home for there is an economic necessity for them to seek employment. In any case, Indian professional women want to work because they desire the independent identity formation, elevated economic status, personal freedom, sense of achievement, and familial respect that employment outside the home makes possible. Thus, except for visa status anxiety in the US, the motivations for work among professional Indian working women resident in India, and those resident in America were very similar. Second, as far as the ideological conditions in the workplace are concerned, professional working women in India appear to face more gender discrimination than those in the US because anti-discrimination legislation is not so stringently enforced in India. Third, there is social interaction with colleagues among the interviewees living in India than among subjects resident in the US. This may be because Indians who have left their homeland have a harder time penetrating social cliques in America both at work and outside, than those who stayed behind in India. Lastly, interviewees in India shied away from discussing friendships or even casual social interactions with male colleagues. In fact, in contrast to the subjects in the US, these women gave the impression that they avoided all socialization with workmates of the opposite sex.

AMERICAN WORKPLACE AND SELF/IDENTITY FORMATION

There are many benefits for Asian Indian women working in the US. Their salary enables them to support themselves and their families. Separation from their families in India, racial prejudice, and social unease in the new American environment are tolerated in order to achieve a higher standard of living than would have been possible in India. However expensive they may be, access to consumer goods, home ownership, and a good education for children are of paramount importance to Indian immigrants. The women's economic contributions help their families to reach these goals, which in turn enhances the prestige of the women within the family, resulting in an increase in decision-making power and a positive self-image.

Working outside the home in paid employment has other advantages: firstly, it allows Asian Indian women to become acculturated into the mainstream of American society, thus, the woman are more comfortable (than before acculturation) in their adopted country of residence. Secondly, even though they are not as vocal in this regard as they might have been, over the years the emphasis on equality between the sexes in American culture inspires women to demand equality at home, weakening the hold of patriarchal values on Asian Indian women. This is a positive step in the direction of independent identity formation.

However, participation in the American workforce is not without costs. My subjects stressed that they worked in professional environments, in high-tech positions, and in highly-respected occupation. However, like all working women in the US, they were affected by the wage-gap between men and women in the US. Moreover, since they were no longer protected from racial and ethnic prejudice by the four walls of their home, Asian Indian women experienced social exclusion in the workplace and realized that they were unlikely to be accepted as 'one of us' by Americans. Thus, Shupriya, one of the subjects of this study said:

I don't think that Americans see me as an American. Maybe they all know that I have been here a long time . . . but when they come to my house they always want to have Indian food. So they obviously don't see me as an American.

The greatest challenge to identity is that though Indian immigrants identify with the White American majority, as Homi Bhabha has pointed out,

Americans 'misrecognize' them as 'others', that is, ethnic difference is what is noticed the most. Most mainstream Americans do not acknowledge the Americanness of Indian immigrants as much as the latter would like.

Minorities often morph into what the majority community perceives them to be. When Indian immigrant women interact with Americans at work (and also in wider American society) they realize that they are perceived primarily as 'ethnic representatives of India', and they then feel compelled to emphasize that part of their persona. Yet, fear of being penalized for being different at work necessitates efforts at continuing to act American at work. For instance, Mrigakshi, one of the interviewees in this study explained that there are almost no Indians at her workplace, so she cannot go in salwar kameez or sari, she always wears Western clothes to work.

Thus, the only space for enacting what they now believe is the most important part of their identity—the Indian immigrant—is in the home. Ironically then, the show of being Indian takes place in a site removed from where the impetus for acting Indian arises: the American workplace. The audience for this performance is largely the women themselves, for they come to believe that the most important component of their personality is their Indianness. In addition, there is pressure from within the immigrant community on women to behave in a more Indian (ethnicized, traditional, and subservient) fashion. This pressure also forces immigrant women to be more Indian, especially at home and in community events, than they would have perhaps been otherwise. The decision to be traditional at home moves Asian Indian woman back to their traditional (subordinate) role within the patriarchal Indian family and the traditional self-sacrificing family-centred female self is constructed. This trend contradicts and coexists with the impulse for gender equity forwarded by female employment and Western, specifically American feminism present within general American society and the American workplace.

Despite exaggerated Indianness at home, Asian Indian working women are scared of being targeted for being different and so they try to follow the American model as closely as possible at work. Sometimes, they are called upon to 'represent' their ethnicity at work too, that is, when they are asked specific questions about India and Indians. Of course, at such times, Indian immigrant working women are able to demonstrate their ethnicity at work too, but such occasions are exceptional. On the whole, Indian immigrant working women are American in the workplace and Indian at home.

This produces a conflicted self. It creates dissonance within the self and it chips away at the women's sense of being integrated consistent people, which, following Claude Steele, I will assume to be a psychological need. Steele's theories help to explain how women deal with these challenges to the integrity of the self, and will be discussed more fully in Chapter III.

CONCLUSION

In this chapter I have discussed various factors including race, gender, and social interaction in the workplace, as well as employment retention, advancement, and termination in the lives of immigrant Indian women in the Bay Area. Comparisons were made between the work-related experiences of Indian immigrant women who work outside the home in paid employment and their counterparts who stayed on in India. I found that while my subjects did complain of isolated incidents of gender bias in the American workplace, they acknowledged that it was less prevalent than it was in India, a fact corroborated by my own data collection in India. While none of my subjects admitted to suffering any incidents of overt racism at work, they did mention that they were left out of social cliques, hence it was more difficult for them to advance to management positions than it was for native-born Americans. I discovered that race was difficult to talk about, since many of my subjects found it humiliating to admit to a racialized existence in the US.

Another notable finding was that Indian American women who work outside the home in paid employment are relatively frank about the importance of the female income for familial economic success. On the other hand, aware of the criticisms of working women in patriarchal India, employed women in India claim that their incomes are useful but inessential. However, I observed that in many cases, the women's financial contribution is vital for attaining the basic comforts considered necessary by the newly globalized Indian middle class that resides in India. I found a surprising global uniformity in the motivations among working women in India and their immigrant counterparts resident in the US. Both groups were driven by the desire for upward economic mobility, status accumulation, expectational conformity, and agency. Immigrant working women were differentiated only by their anxiety about visa status for naturally this was not a concern shared by the Indian working women resident in India. I found that psychological dissonance is caused by contradictions between the American role played at work, and the Indian persona adopted at home. In Chapter III, I will discuss how my subjects resolved this potential threat to the self.

CHAPTER III

*Professional Women at Home
and in the Immigrant Community*

INTRODUCTION

THIS CHAPTER WILL look at the home life and the community presence of Indian immigrant working women in the San Francisco Bay Area, making comparisons with non-working women in the same region, as well as with working women resident in India. The aim is to compare the construction of the self in the home and community of immigrant Indian working women with that of immigrant non-working Indian women in America and working non-immigrant Indian women in India.

CULTURE

WOMEN AS THE BEARERS OF REMIXED
INDIAN CULTURAL HERITAGE

Examining the concept of 'home' in transnational English literature, Rosemary George theorizes that the home is a place of exclusion as well as inclusion, conflict as well as care, and a welcome refuge as well as a prison from which one needs to escape. By extension, the idea of the home is also conflated with ideas of the self (1996). The question of how Indian immigrant homes in the US differ from other homes becomes pertinent for this study. Significantly, the Indian American home is the site of perpetual cultural confrontation, of daily acceptance as well as exclusion of American culture. The Indian diasporic home is where American culture is learnt, but it is also where efforts to rebuild some form of Indian culture take place.

Diasporic Indians are as American as is necessary to succeed in their public life, and with time, innumerable Americanisms such as the overriding need for privacy and individual choice creep into their private lives as well, but yet they are eager to reformulate their native cultural and religious heritage, and they have the freedom and the resources to make this happen in the US. Due to the mass migration of an unprecedented number of people across the globe in recent times, and due to the current proliferation of diasporic or transnational electronic and print mass media, transnationals can now establish a presence in diasporic public spheres. Hence, they can now imagine and maintain a diasporic identity. Minority populations identify with post-national constituencies of religious, ethnic, or linguistic affiliations, rather than confining their selfhood to narrow national boundaries.

Arjun Appadurai has explained that because of its pluralistic beliefs, and because of its pride in being a land of immigrants, the US continues to be the chosen destination for thousands of immigrants. They arrive in America as workers, refugees, or students. Once arrived, they form delocalized transnations whose *raison d'être* originates from a particular geographical location, but which are completely diasporic in nature (1996). Bay Area Indian Americans have been rather successful in the construction of their transnational selves since they have access to numerous electronic and print media that have desi-related content and that are easily accessed at home via the internet/CDs/DVDs/cable TV/desi magazines and newsletters. In addition, since there are many fellow Indian Americans in the Bay Area, desi stores and restaurants are quite popular, and it is relatively easy for members of the desi minority to get-together and create cultural/religious/linguistic/culinary events that serve to reaffirm diasporic desi identity and maintain delocalized Indian American transnations. Hence in the Bay Area, the Indian American home is most definitely a site for cultural reproduction and the diasporic creation of transnational desi identity.

It must be noted here that cultural reproduction has been achieved at the expense of the well-being of many of the female members of the Indian diasporic community. My research among female professional Indian immigrants in the Bay Area has shown that the Indian community in the US has been able to deploy Indian culture in the US only by sacrificing female individuation and autonomy.

Indian immigrant women are idealized by their family and community and expected to be culturally and morally perfect, and so they are stringently reviewed and restricted by the community. Tribhuvan, the husband of one of my interviewees, complained, 'My desi [Indian] colleagues and friends disapprove of my wife Charulata living in Seattle while she completes her Ph.D. work. "Can't she do some studies locally in the Bay Area?" they ask.' The immigrant community enforces the ideal that an Indian woman's place is by her husband's side. Parvati, another subject in my study, says:

My husband comes back from Indian get-togethers and parties and worries about the comments his friends have made about the difficulties of bringing up Indian girls in the United States. As a result, he is very strict with our daughter Moni. He has told me to make sure that she should never go on dates, she should not even go to the local mall with her girlfriends, and of course, now that she is a teenager, sleepovers are out of the question!

In fact, the community's attempts to recreate a monolithic 'traditional' and 'authentic' culture has compelled its women to perpetuate behavioural restraints. These norms are anachronistic not only by American standards, but also by current behavioural standards in India. Indian immigrant families try to rigidly adhere to the values prevalent in India at the time of their departure which may have been several years earlier, and the women are expected to lead this effort.

Yen Le Espiritu has shown that for communities which are economically or politically suppressed, female morality is one of the few spheres in which they can claim superiority. Hence women are constructed as more faithful wives, more dedicated mothers, and more loving daughters than their White counterparts. Ethnic women are idealized as virtuous paragons of sexual restraint and family centred representatives of traditional culture (2003). Shamita Dasgupta argues that the trend of seeing women as emblems of a nation's cultural survival is a direct descendant of the medieval Indian tradition of depositing family honor, *izzat*, in its female members (1998). Indian diasporic women are expected to safeguard the family's *izzat* by rigidly controlling their own as well as their daughter's desires and actions.

Dasgupta has shown that the Indian community expects Indian immigrant mothers to Indianize their children, especially their daughters. However, community pressure is not the sole cause of Indianization of the second generation. From deep within their own individual psyches, the mothers themselves feels urges to acculturate their daughters in the same traditions with which they grew up.

Sucheta Mazumdar emphasizes that in the Indian diasporic community, women are regarded as the repositories and transmitters of Indian culture. For example, at formal social events, Indian women wear traditional clothing, but Indian immigrant men invariably wear Western suits. Even at non-Indian gatherings, Indian women give a touch of exotic diversity by wearing saris or salwar kameezes, but Indian men prefer formal Western attire. 'Women are forever the bearers of culture, the preservers of heritage; they must after all look the part' (1996: 467).

Interviews and participant observation confirmed that the subjects of this study retained Indian culture in their clothes, food choices, and religio-cultural practices more than their male counterparts. This gendered division of cultural representation can be seen in India as well. The women wear saris, salwar kameezes, or kurtis at desi parties but more often than not, the men wear shirt and trouser ensembles on such occasions. Many ate only vegetarian food, even while their husbands and children ate eggs, fish, chicken, and lamb. The women cooked Indian food, but the men did not do so often. Female immigrants performed puja more often than their male counterparts and they regularly fasted on religious occasions, even though the men rarely did so. While both men and women were involved in the cultural productions of music and dance, more women than men participated in such shows.

In agreement with my findings, Meera Srinivas notes that it is the women in the Indian immigrant community who uphold Indian traditions. They are the ones who make time for Indian music classes, puja, ethnic clothes, and native language studies (Srinivas 2001). Srinivas argues persuasively that Indian diasporic men are culturally inactive in comparison to the women.

Transmission of cultural beliefs and practices to the new generation is important to immigrant parents, but it is not possible in the new country unless a reformulation, reformation or renewal of ethnic culture is undertaken in the new location. Thus, following cultural formulae learnt in the homeland, new cultural institutions, spaces, and occasions are created in the country of settlement in order to revive the languages, cultural practices, culinary recipes, fashions, and religious rites of the country of birth. Indian immigrant women drive the majority of the cultural recreation in the country of settlement. Since women tend to spend more time with the children than the men do, they are naturally assigned the role of a transmitter of Indian cultural traditions to the next generation. Sangeeta, a part-time preschool teacher, says:

My husband is hardly at home. He has his regular job and he has also taken up some teaching assignments in a local university. I don't even get to see him on Saturdays, besides the usual work week he usually works Saturdays too, so I spend all my time with my son, and I have taught him to read and write Tamil. I have also taught him many songs in our language.

Vijaylakshmi, a non-working wife and mother says, 'My husband Vikram returns from work at 8.30 p.m. every night. So I have to keep my son busy single-handedly most of the evening. It is almost his bedtime by the time my husband returns home. I am trying to teach him Sanskrit *slokas*.' Most of the women complained bitterly of the long hours that their husbands spent at work, and how they spent most of their time alone with their children. Since these women spend the most time with their children, they are in charge of the children's cultural training. Rani says, 'My husband travels a lot, but I make sure the children eat an Indian dinner every night. My husband is south Indian, and he wants the children to eat *sambhar* and rice, and they do.' Chitra and Lakshmi both take their children to Hindu scripture classes at Chinmaya Mission every Sunday. Urmila takes her daughter to classes at Swaranjali, a school of north Indian music and dance, although her son is taken to weekend basketball games by his father. Vijaylakshmi spends an hour doing puja every day, and she says she wants to teach her son the importance of puja by demonstrating her own commitment to it. Her husband is passionate about safeguarding his family's Hindu traditions, but he has no time for puja, hence Vijaylakshmi must be the preserver and transmitter of Hinduism (although so far, her son has shown little interest).

Though Indian men are secondarily involved in cultural production, they are also important in the effort to reformulate Indian culture in the US, for it is they who set the course, they are the ones who are the first to emphasize the need to mobilize Indian culture at home. While it is the men's will to be Indian at home, it is the women who carry out this policy. Tathagata says:

I think as an Indian immigrant father it is my duty to acquaint my children with Indian culture. If I will not introduce my children to Indian culture, then who else will do it? Their environment is totally American, so at home we introduce them to Indian culture. Once they grow up, it is their choice, they can choose whichever culture they want, Indian or American, but at least they will have the choice.

Ashesh says he wants his son to meet a Swamiji he respects immensely:

We are going to visit the Vivekananda Mission in Los Angeles during the Christmas break. We used to go there regularly when we lived in LA. We respect the Swamiji there very much. We haven't seen him since we moved to the Bay Area. We want to pay our respects to the Swamiji, and we also want our son to meet with the Swamiji.

Similarly, Harishchandra insists that his wife Pramiti should wear saris at work and that his daughter Tripti should speak in Hindi at home. Abhay is equally vehement in his views. He says, 'I have told Parvati [his wife] "No Hindi films are to be watched in our home, only Telegu films"'. Bankim wants his daughter Anshula to speak in her mother tongue Bengali, not English. He says of his daughter, 'When she speaks English at home, I get very irritated, aamar gaa jole jaye (my body burns with anger)'. Arjun says, 'Our daughter must be given an opportunity to acquaint herself with Indian culture'. While he spends most of his weekends playing golf, he does make time to take his daughter to Bharatnatyam (south Indian dance) classes. His wife Kalyani does puja and fasts for Hanumanji, the Monkey God, every Tuesday; she says, 'I hope my puja makes an impression on our daughter, but to tell you the truth, despite my efforts, she has not really taken any interest in it'. One might speculate that even if left to themselves, the women would have come up with a similar India-centric family policy, but perhaps they would have been more lenient than their husbands. Arunima says, 'My husband does not even approve of Hindi film culture for the kids, let alone American culture, but I am OK with Hindi film culture. He likes only Bengali, he teaches them Bengali script over the weekends.'

Cultural Authenticity

Though women in the diasporic community have been charged with perpetuating so-called 'traditional' Indian culture in the land of settlement, I have doubts about the authenticity of the culture disseminated in the US. It should be noted that because all cultures are continually evolving, all claims of cultural authenticity must be examined very carefully. That which is propagated in the name of Indian culture in the US can hardly claim to represent the diversity of Indian culture, or current transformations of lived culture in India. Indian food, language, and religion are essential cultural blocks that allow immigrants to get a taste of their native culture in the land of settlement. However, Indian culture as practiced and presented in the Indian American community tends to be a random jumble of either garish Bollywood song and dance routines, or adulterated versions of centuries old classical Indian music, dance, and theatre that the youth cannot connect to, or discordant modern counterparts that the older generation of immigrants cannot relate to. Espiritu says that native culture is essentialized in the US as a simplified constant, and it does not account for the complexities of cultural change and indeterminacy in the nation of origin (2003). While ethnic culture perpetuated in the Indian immigrant home is often outdated and over-simplified, essentialization of culture for the sake of public displays of ethnic and cultural unity is the hallmark of the Indian American community. In Shamita Dasgupta's opinion, the 'powerful of the communities' leaders have endeavoured to create counterfeit authenticity by denying culture's essential flux and inherent disparities' (1998).

Racial Chauvinism

One of my subjects, Shupriya, observed that Indians are racial chauvinists:

Most Indians wouldn't want their kids to marry anyone outside the community, but if it has to be, then White is better . . . A lot of my friends' kids are of marriageable age . . . I find parents here are much more strict and unreasonable than parents back there [in India]. I really do. And it is amazing . . . . [This is] because they are so scared their kids will marry someone outside the community . . . it is just fear of the unknown....[They say] 'Ora bhalo noy (They are bad).'

I too have noticed a tendency for racial exclusion in the Indian immigrant community in the Bay Area, especially a negative attitude towards Blacks and Hispanics. In fact, Mazumdar has observed that most first generation Indian immigrants identify with the White middle class in America, even though they are not always accepted by it. Primed by their colonial history of worship of the *gora log* (White man), Indian immigrant bourgeoisie easily mimic Anglo-European dominant culture, hope for upward mobility, and seldom explore Asian linkages. The state and other established powers in the US find it useful to accept the alliance of the Indian immigrant middle class for like other 'model minority' communities, Indian Americans are given the task of disciplining blue-collar Blacks and Hispanics. As a 'model minority', Indians in North America avoid any mention of domestic violence, child abuse, homosexuality, or the rising divorce rate within the community; they prefer to hold forth on superior Indian family values. Mazumdar writes that the South Asian middle class shares one common goal with the White middle class: that of ensuring the cultural and political hegemony of the bourgeoisie. However, unlike the socially secure Euro-American middle class, it knows that its social conservatism and material success cannot ensure a place in the American middle class. Therefore, members of the Indian American community reinvent themselves, Americanizing their accent, clothes, hair styles, and names in order to fit in. They walk a tightrope between Westernization and maintenance of ethnic cultural 'authenticity' (1996).

Keya Ganguly affirms that Indian immigrants are aware of their marginality—they are 'not quite White', and hence, 'not quite right'. Reconciled to the impossibility of becoming American (or even Americanized) on account of their anomalous appearance, accent, religion, and culture, they redirect their psychic and material energies into communal and cultural productions which acquire the status of cultural rituals. Self-fashioning becomes the only path to self-authentication (2001).

Parents and First Generation Indian American Children: A Clash of Cultures

Most of the Indian American children and youth I interacted with were eager to become fully Americanized. However, despite their offspring's lack of interest in Indian habits and traditions, Indian immigrant parents exert themselves to expose their children to Indian culture. 'American Born Confused Desis' (ABCDs) is a term used to distinguish Indian Americans born and raised in the US from those Indian Americans who were born and brought up in India and immigrated as adults. The 'Indianization' of the ABCDs by their Indian-born parents may take the form of forcing the children to speak the Indian language and eat Indian food at home, or it may include frequent vacations to India to visit family, or it might consist of Indian dance, music, language, or religious lessons over the weekends.

This study has shown that each Indian immigrant family does have its own individual method of balancing American assimilation with the deployment of Indian culture. In fact, many families are much more flexible about cultural choices than communities as a whole.

Jean Bacon has stated:

> Whatever a family has to say about being Indian grows out of the way its members lead their lives. Families do not seem very concerned with living up to ideas about Indianness. In the absence of this ideational aspect of adjustment, family life exists on the boundaries between Indian and American and consequently is free to exhibit wide variations and highly idiosyncratic patterns of interaction and adjustment. (1996: 249)

It is surprising that Bacon argues that families do not care whether they live up to ideas of Indianness, for this research reveals that almost every family is concerned about maintaining a degree of Indianness even if only in some spheres. Since it is impossible to be all-Indian while resident in America, families tend to focus on particular areas of cultural enactment within the family. These areas often include the restriction of their daughters' interaction with males (especially Black or Hispanic males), religious rituals, consumption of Indian and often vegetarian food, and female family members donning Indian clothes for Indian gatherings. Indian immigrant mothers bear the responsibility of inculcating Indian values and behavioural norms in their children.

As Manisha Roy explains, the young Indian immigrant wife enjoys breaking free from the fetters of the joint family and age-old Indian traditions and she is happy to be the undisputed mistress of her home. However, as the children become more and more Americanized, particularly in adolescence, then the mother insists that they should not forget the food, language, and traditions of their mother's own Indian past (1998: 104). In my opinion, the Indian immigrant mother's restrictive reaction to the Americanization of her children is not only a typical parental fear of peer-pressure driven teenage misbehaviour, but also a hope that a traditional Indian upbringing will result in a respect for their country of origin among immigrant youth.

Religious Frameworks in the US

It is often observed that immigrant community leaders attempt to recreate a semblance of the religious and cultural framework that they left behind in India. They build temples, gurdwaras, and mosques in order to regain any status lost due to dislocation from their homeland. They tend to be far more engaged with ethno-religious activism in the US than they ever were in India. Mazumdar states that white-collar Indian immigrants, about whom my work is concerned, are known to be religious in the US. On a related note, she also affirms that the growing population of working class Indian immigrants in the US, such as cab-drivers, cooks, janitors, store cashiers, waiters, gas station attendants, and motel workers is also fiercely religious. They support the religio-cultural glorification of Indian heritage propogated by community leaders who themselves want nothing to do with blue-collar immigrants. Lacking the professional qualifications necessary for local white-collar employment, many immigrants are forced to take working class jobs which they abhor. These are immigrants whose skills do not match what is required in American white-collar jobs. Many of these underskilled Indian immigrants may have come to the US as family members of more accomplished primary immigrants. Regenerating their national and religious identity allows them to claim moral and racial superiority over those who tend to lie at the bottom of the social hierarchy: Blacks and Latinos (1996).

LACK OF INCLUSIVENESS

In general, the idea of a community implies amicable inclusion of people with whom one has something in common, and perhaps, exclusion of those with whom one has little in common. The members of the community of Indian Americans in the Bay Area share many similarities. However, let alone empathy with all those outside the community, relations even between members of the community are not always harmonious. Urmila says she is proud that Indians in the Bay Area are generally in professional occupations. She is a physician and she says that Indian doctors are generally respected in the Bay Area for they are known to be very competent. Urmila was distressed to see that in the UK, the first thing she noticed on arrival was the prevalence of Indian sweeper women at Heathrow Airport. Urmila expressed concern that many of the new Indian immigrants in the Bay Area are not professionals, but rather, they are unskilled labourers. For example, she has recently come across many Indian taxi drivers in San Francisco. Urmila is worried about this trend for she would prefer that Americans in the Bay Area think of Indian immigrants as highly qualified professionals, not as uneducated or semi-educated labourers.

Mindful of its professional and upwardly mobile majority, the Indian community in the Bay Area is determined to project a middle class image. It therefore puts a lot of pressure on its members to acquire the financial trappings of the American middle class. Home ownership, buying new cars, expensive college education and lavish birthday, *annaprasanam*, graduation, and wedding celebrations for their children are all required if one wants to escape criticism from fellow Indians. This is especially true in the Bay Area because a lot of Indians have made millions of dollars in the high-tech industry. Kalyani, a teacher, stated that:

We live in a rented house. My Bay Area resident so-called friends here are always asking me, 'So when are you going to buy a house?' They tell me of all their problems with their maids; now why tell me, what will I do knowing all that? The truth is, they just want to make me feel small because I can't afford to buy a house or hire a maid.

Charulata, a web designer who has not yet managed to buy a home says, 'Those who have millions [of dollars] in the desi community, you know, a million dollar home, and a string of brand new expensive cars in their driveway, they have already written us off, they don't talk to us anymore'. Her husband, a computer programmer, says:

I hate that everyone I interact with in the Indian community only talks of coding and programming, or buying a house or car, not of politics or art or culture, or even of writing papers in journals. I am an exception in my company, I try to publish my research results in the appropriate scientific journals, I have twelve journal publications.

Indians in the Bay Area, especially first generation immigrants, are not only class conscious, they are also ethnically insular. They can afford to be ethnically exclusive because there are so many fellow-Indian immigrants and so many Indian resources in the Bay Area that they do not have to depend on non-Indian social contacts, cultural artefacts, and communitarian resources. This makes it difficult for Indians married to non-Indians to make friends within the Indian community. Aditi White is the young wife of a senior American professor in a university in San Francisco. She says, 'We come across many Indians, but it is difficult to find people on the same wavelength. In fact, ever since I came here five years ago, only one Indian family has invited us to their home.'

Organizations that highlight some of the dissensions which the community labours to deny, such as groups that work with victims of domestic violence (Narika and Maitri), gays and lesbians (Trikone), and mistakenly targeted Sikh taxi drivers, are often dismissed from community parades and other performances of community identity. Mazumdar explains that Indian diasporic leaders collude with the American state in the preservation of the status quo:

Control of these little sanction slots for displaying 'heritage' and national cultures, marching in parades, and deciding who will be allowed to participate in the 'international fairs', legitimizes the immigrant bourgeoisie's social and political standing among other immigrants in the community. (1996: 464)

Due to intra-community peer pressure, the appearance of a homogeneous community is maintained not only publicly, but also privately. In homes, families, and marriages, differences are actively repressed by a call for 'cultural purity'. As Shamita Dasgupta has written, being loyal to the traditional culture in private as well as public, 'is an immigrant's ticket to belonging' (1998: 5).

Despite these criticisms of the Indo-American community, the novelist Chitra Divakaruni, who is also the founder of a South Asian women's help line Maitri, praises the increasingly liberal mentality of the Indian community in the Bay Area: 'The attitude of the Indian community to the issue of domestic abuse and an organization like Maitri has really changed in the last ten years. Now Indians seem to realize that the problem of domestic abuse needs to be resolved and Maitri is here to help do that' (personal meeting 2001). It seems that American progressiveness has had a hand in changing inequitable gender relations among Indians in the US, but more importantly, the expanding feminist movement in mainland India has spurred immigrant Indians to correct excesses of gender discrimination within the diasporic community. Indian feminism has influenced the younger generation of middle class Indian women in the homeland to a great extent. When they immigrate to America, these young women bring their feminist ideals with them, and in many cases, they join Maitri, Narika, and other Bay Area organizations that assist victims of domestic abuse within the Indian overseas community.

Language Usage

There are many private language schools in the Bay Area that teach the Indian regional languages. An important issue in the reformulation of traditional Indian culture in diasporic Indian homes is the choice of language spoken at home. First generation Indo-American immigrants have different degrees of comfort when speaking in their Indian mother tongue and with English. Naturally, the more comfortable the family members are in the Indian native language, and the less comfortable they are in English, the more the Indian language is spoken at home. Abhay admits that even after many years in the US, he is still more comfortable speaking Telugu than English. His English fails him occasionally:

Coming to this country, I have learnt English, but Telugu is my own language. I learnt only Telugu as a child. I grew up in Shubham village. When I got admission in IIT then I had to learn Hindi. My classmates at IIT used to laugh at my pathetic attempts to speak Hindi. Here I speak in English at work, but in times of crisis, Telugu still comes to my lips, not English. I was in court the other day, and for fully fifteen seconds my English failed me, and I found myself blurting out Telugu.

He and his wife speak Telugu to each other at home, and they also speak Telugu when conversing with their adolescent children, even though the children always reply in English.

At the other end of the spectrum we have Dr Urmila Sarkar and Mrinalini, both of whom had a very Westernized upbringing in India. Dr Sarkar explained:

Tushar and I rarely speak in Bengali. The children both spoke Bengali and understood really well when they were small, but once they started preschool, they switched to English, and now they chatter away in English. Then we chatter in English to them. It's like a bad habit. It's because we feel very comfortable in English. It's basically like almost a first language for us. So it is a bit of a problem.

Mrinalini says:

I try to speak to my daughter in Malayalam, but since I am used to speaking in English, often English comes naturally to me, and I have to consciously force myself to speak in Malayalam so that she can pick up some Malayalam from me. My husband grew up outside Kerala, so he is not at all fluent in Malayalam, so he always speaks in English.

This study has shown that the tendency to use the mother tongue at home is conditioned by the parents' access to the language. Depending of their upbringing and schooling, my interviewees were fluent in their native language and in English in varying degrees. They were aware that learning the mother tongue is important for their children, but not all of them succeeded in teaching it. Despite their parents' efforts, Indian American children are reluctant to speak in their mother tongue.

Women's Empowerment: Cultural Deployment, Female Employment, and Agency

The degree of female empowerment varies according to different communities, classes, and income brackets. Normally professional Indian working women enjoyed more rights and resources than non-working women in the Indian diasporic community of the San Francisco Bay Area. However, non-working women reported that they believed that their agency and status in the household had improved upon migration out of India.

Despite the increase in agency, the status of immigrant Indian women was still not comparable to that of their men at home and within the ethnic community as ethnic traditions dictate against gender equity. In Meera Syal's novel, *Life Isn't All Haa Haa Hee Hee*, the heroine Tanya writes of her Punjabi immigrant mother settled in the UK: 'Mum was heavier than the rest of the family's combined weight. . . . But she shriveled to the size of a pea around her husband' (2000: 143). Syal insists that even though an earned income improves the status of women in the Indian immigrant home, this improvement is only to a certain extent:

I've seen enough to recognize it for what it is, our collective shameful secret, we meet the world head up, head on, we meet our men and we bow down gratefully, cling to compromise like a lover who promises all will be well if we don't make trouble. We hear our mother's voices and heed them, to make up for all the other imagined transgressions in our lives (2000: 145–6).

Syal paints a rather dismal picture of the woman's position in the Indian immigrant home but the accuracy of such a portrayal can be questioned. I think that while Syal may have captured the tone of the majority of male-female relationships in the Indian immigrant community, her value judgements give them a pathos and sense of backwardness that the women concerned would not have necessarily associated with their own lives. Syal's caricature of Indian womanhood is unintentionally reinforced by Parmatma Saran, an Indian immigrant author. Unlike Syal, Saran approves of what he characterizes as typical non-assertive behaviour of Indian women, 'Generally, Indian women are less assertive than their American counterparts and the majority feel that relations cannot be changed by being too assertive. They recognize that being too assertive and demanding is not the right approach to correct things' (1985: 97). In this day and age Saran's view on the 'right approach' seems quite indefensible.

The observations above point to the far-reaching influence of the upbringing of an individual prior to migration. It is difficult to disassociate a person from the paradigm which formed the basis of his or her upbringing. The nature of upbringing in the nation of origin, that is, India, is responsible for a large part of identity formation and self-perception of Indian immigrant women in the US.

Education, Westernization, and middle class idealism have all acted to vastly improve the status of women in the highly-educated, elite, middle class families from whence Indian professional female immigrants to the US tend to originate. However, liberal idealism about male-female equality found among parents, siblings, friends, and teachers cannot completely hide the still prevalent male chauvinist attitudes of portions of the Indian nation. Also, while many progressive parents in India might want to bring up their daughters in a non-sexist manner, their own more conservative parents usually try to discourage such efforts. In general, sexism is ingrained in the Indian psyche and it is impossible for an Indian woman, however progressive her immediate family or friends might be, to escape it. Equally, in many cases, neither Indian middle class idealism, nor American feminism can totally rid Indian woman of certain backward chauvinistic ideas such as these.

Given these drawbacks, the successful careers of some Indian women are remarkable. Indian women have been especially successful in the spheres of academics, medicine, computer software writing, law, and politics.

American feminists such as Sylvia Yanagisako, proclaim that gender differences that are portrayed as natural must be revealed to be what they really are: differences and inequalities constructed by culture (Yanagisako and Delaney 1995). Feminist, liberal, and progressive sensibilities suggest that Indian immigrant women in the US, even the majority of those who are educated and professionally or semi-professionally qualified working women, are traditional in their thinking. Contrary to the ideas of Western feminism delineated so clearly by feminists such as Yanagisako, Indian immigrant women in the US seem to cling to the concept of essentialist gender differences, such as the ideal of the woman as nurturer, and the man as protector. They hesitate to dismiss such stereotypes as inequalities constructed by culture. In general, due to these discrepancies in opinion, Indian immigrant women seem conflicted about whether to follow Western feminists, home-grown Indian feminists, or anti-feminist Indian traditionalists.

Childcare and housework are two of the contentious issues which are affected by ideas of what ideal womanhood should be. Indian immigrant working women do not hesitate to avail themselves of the excellent childcare facilities in America and employed Indian immigrant women invariably put their children in professional childcare within six to twelve weeks of birth, that being the state-approved length of maternity leave. Rather than opting for culturally alien American daycare centres or expensive American nannies, many Indian immigrant couples in the Bay Area put their children in South Asian childcare centres, or the grandparents spend six month alternating stints in the US so that the newborn child is cared for in a home environment by co-ethnics or relatives in the first year of life. Unlike Arlie Hochschild's American interviewees, Indian immigrant working wives in Bay Area did not make very serious attempts to pressure their husbands to increase their share of housework and childcare. Instead, they employ domestic help and childcare providers to lighten the burden (1989).

Childcare and housework are however not the only issues. Gender roles are fairly rigid in India and those husbands who fail to excel in their careers experience shame, as do their wives. An Indian immigrant wife may earn enough to support her husband and children, but she feels humiliated on account of her husband's failure to succeed in his career. Some of the subjects of this study gave examples of how they had had to make some sacrifices in their own careers in order to give primacy to that of their husband. Two of the women interviewed had even given up promising jobs in order to relocate to areas where their husband had found good employment. Mitul, a postdoctoral researcher in the social sciences explains: 'I obtained a tenure track teaching job in an Ivy League university right after I completed my Ph.D., but my husband could not find any work there. He was offered a position in San Francisco, and so we have moved here. I found a research position soon after we came here, and I have no regrets, since both of us love our work and also, we can be together.' This self-sacrificing desire on the part of female Indian immigrants to give priority to male careers is one which most feminists would condemn.

Most Asian Indian women, even those who call themselves feminists, hesitate to make alliances with Western feminists. Indian American feminists such as C.T. Mohanty fault Western feminism for reducing all problems of inequity to a single denominator, that of gender. Mohanty claims that Western feminists are not sensitive to issues of race, class, and colonial domination. Sometimes Western feminists do concern themselves with 'third world women', meaning all women of, and originating from, the developing world, including those that are living in the developed world. However, Western feminists often fail to recognize the heterogeneity of these women of the developing world. Mohanty claims that many Western feminists stereotype all these women as 'backward victims' who may need to be rescued by the 'progressive and liberal' women of the West (1991).

The ethnographic data in my work will not support generalizations about Western and Indian feminism, but I do want to argue that this study has revealed that on the whole, most Indian immigrant women are conservative in their thinking and they are hesitant to join Western feminists, or feminists of any sort at all. I have observed that whether they are employed in service or manufacturing positions, or whether they are entrepreneurial, Indian immigrant working women seem to have one thing in common: they are determined to retain male/patriarchal superiority within the family, or at least a semblance of it. This remains the case despite the fact that their contribution to the family income renders them capable of breaking out of patriarchal oppression should they desire.

As mentioned earlier in this chapter, I met with the eminent writer and women's rights activist Chitra Divakaruni in a personal meeting at her home. She is President of Maitri, a South Asian women's helpline. Critical of the position of women in the Indian immigrant community, she explains: 'Many women who came to Maitri need to know simple things like opening a bank account or getting citizenship. Some of them had lived in America for decades but knew no life outside their homes'. However, I believe that all evaluations of a woman's empowerment are relative to the position she may have been in had she not immigrated. The women interviewed for this study were happy with the freedoms they had won in their own lives even if perceptions of what they could have achieved do not meet with the reality of their position.

All the women quoted above report a certain basic satisfaction with the life they lead in the US and the comfort level with the way they have organized their lives seems to be uniform whether the women are unemployed, employed part-time, or employed full-time. A key reason for this is that most of them feel that they have made gains in individuation and personal freedom because of their immigration to the US. To US-born women, the lives of first generation immigrant Indian women may seem restricted and bound by patriarchal traditions, but the women themselves often feel that they have gained significant freedoms simply by virtue of the fact that they have settled in the US. Such freedoms include: the capacity to study for degrees from world-renowned US universities; working with the best facilities modern technology can offer; mixing with people of cultures they had only read about or heard about before migrating out of India; the ability to drive a car and go out by themselves; the ability to earn salaries that allow the purchase of previously unattainable consumer items and vacation packages that were out of reach in India; freedom from day-to-day interference from meddlesome neighbours and distant relatives in the extended marital and natal families; and the replacement of traditional patriarchal spousal relations with a more 'companionate' model. These may seem to be modest gains to some, but they are still considerable in the eyes of the women who experience them. Though male chauvinistic pressures from conservative forces within the overseas Indian community, and the reification of a traditional Indian identity due to perceived rejection by so-called mainstream Americans, do often result in a continuation of patriarchal behaviours, there is substantial post-migrational progression towards a more equitable reconfiguration of gender relations.

The majority of the Indian immigrant professional and semi-professional women interviewed for this study experienced degrees of empowerment in their personal and marital lives. Unlike their counterparts in India, they did not have to deal directly with their extended families or intrusive neighbours on a daily basis. This freed up a lot of time and enabled them to devote this time to pursue their own interests. Though the immigrant community often attempted to restrict the women's so-called Americanized individuation, as previously discussed, and though, the women themselves wanted to return to an Indian (and hence gender-specific) identity under certain circumstances, the physical distance from their extended family served to enhance their personal decision-making powers. In addition, professional achievement gave these women a sense of achievement and confidence that emboldened them to empower themselves and to resist any oppressive forces. However, I must clarify that my respondents did not always choose such a path of resistance.

Most of the working women spoken to had access to household resources such as a joint bank account and the family car. They decide their own career path, and were co-opted in decision-making regarding, for example, whether or not to start a family, when to have children, and how many, etc. They buy consumer items for personal use, and their input is considerable in making family decisions concerning purchases of consumer goods for the household. The women spoken to also had substantial say in deciding what to do in their leisure time, the timing and destination of vacations, whom to socialize with, and what to wear on what occasion. They yielded significant influence in deciding what school their children would study in, what after-school activities the children would engage in, and whom to hire to help with housework and childcare. Also, though housework and childcare primarily remain the woman's responsibility, the husbands of working Indian immigrant women do help with a few household chores. Moreover, working Indian immigrant women are free to spend their salaries on lavish gift-giving when visiting their friends and family in India.

Having written about the modest gains in personal freedom that even non-working Indian immigrant women have achieved as a result of immigration, and having discussed the limited but significant empowerment of most working Indian immigrant women, this work will now turn to some of the great improvements in self-sufficiency and leadership that a few working Indian women have achieved in their professional as well as personal lives. Among the Indian professional and semi-professional Indian immigrant women interviewed in the Bay Area, there were a few who had mustered the courage to reinvent the traditional Indian male-female equation. In such cases, Dasgupta's claim on behalf of a section of Indian American immigrant women that 'Passive or insulated womanhood is not our reality' (1998: 3) rings true. In fact, six of my subjects, Smita, Megha, Urmila, Rani, Harjinder, and Niharika, were primary immigrants. They continue to work, but only two of them remain the primary breadwinners for their families. They have progressive views on gender relations, and their families are clearly more concerned about their opinions than the families of many of my other subjects. As Sheba Mariam George points out, many professional Indian women such as nurses are primary immigrants to the US so they sponsor their families to the US, and help them to establish themselves. They continue to be the primary breadwinners and so naturally, they are able to establish equitable gender relations at home and authority within their community (2005).

Having left her two-year-old son in the care of her husband and parents-in-law in Delhi, Smita came to the US on a B1 visa. After arriving in the US, she managed to get an H-1B visa for herself within six months. She then brought her husband and child to the US as her dependents. Smita works as a highly paid independent contractor. She earns as much as $150 per hour as an independent consultant because her expertise is in the much-in-demand field of Oracle software and electronic data interchange. While her earning power and visa sponsoring ability was welcomed by her devoted and down to earth husband, it created some confusion for him and the extended family as Smita challenged the gender norms of her family and society. In fact Smita continued to be the principal wage-earner while her husband continued his education in information technology and ultimately set up a computer software startup enterprise. After ten years in the US, she is still the primary provider for her family, she has been able help provide for her younger brother's education in management, and also takes care of the expenditure for her parents to visit the US annually. Hence Smita has not only challenged gender norms but also been successful enough to support her conjugal as well as her natal family. As a consequence of her own empowerment, Smita has succeeded in establishing what Sheba Mariam George calls 'connective autonomy' by maintaining and strengthening her relationship with various favoured family members by fulfilling mainly financial obligations to them (2005).

Megha is the main provider in her household. She came to the US as an international student and having completed her graduate studies, she is now an associate professor. Her husband is a consultant at a university, but Megha's earning power and visibility (by virtue of her high profile university position) in the Indian community can be seen by some as a disruptive force that challenges the Indian norm of the woman being the 'home-maker'. Megha explains that her husband does the greater portion of the housework, and he is progressive enough to take his 'unmanly' domestic duties in his stride. Thus, Megha and her husband are proud of the level of democratization they have achieved within the moral framework of their family.

Urmila came to study medicine in the US and she is now a physician and owns two private clinics from which she obtains a substantial income. Urmila has developed friendships with many of her Indian immigrant patients and most of them have become family friends. She meets a lot of people by virtue of her work as a physician, and many of her patients are Indian immigrants. She is quite prominent in the Indian American community in the Bay Area, and in certain social circles, more people know her than her husband, who is a successful financial management consultant. Thus, Urmila exercises the autonomy she has gained from successful participation in the labour force by establishing and maintaining social connections with patients/friends. Like Smita does with her natal family, Urmila strengthens ties to her patients-cum-friends, so like Smita, she also demonstrates her empowerment by fulfilling the principle of 'connective autonomy', or a 'self fundamentally understood only within relationships and obligations' (George 2005: 76).

What is remarkable in the lives of these women is the ability they have exhibited to break out of the traditional Indian mould of a wife whose career and ambitions should always be secondary to those of her husband's. They have proved that women are just as capable of being the primary provider not just for themselves, but also for their families.

Aside from the Indian immigrant women in the Bay Area who have made a name for themselves in their respective professions, there are also several who have received local media attention for their achievements. Being more prominent than their husbands in the public eye, these women have obtained a considerable level of empowerment, although they do continue to emphasize their efforts to balance their family lives with their professional careers.

Radha Basu, a first generation Indian immigrant woman who arrived in the US at the age of 21 to study for a Master's Degree in computer science in a Southern Californian university, is by now well known as a pioneer in the software industry in the Silicon Valley. Starting her career in research and development in the area of ultrasound imaging in Hewlett Packard, a company that is acknowledged to be the symbolic founder of the Silicon Valley, Basu went on to setting up Hewlett Packard's first software subsidiaries in Bangalore and Chennai in the mid-1980s. Later, she accepted the position of Chairman and CEO of SupportSoft, a Bay Area based company noted for its trail-blazing work in automated technical support software and activation of consumer broadband offering. Basu held this position till 2006, and received many awards as the CEO of one of the fastest growing companies in the Silicon Valley including the Top 25 Women in the Web Award in February 2000 and the Women of Achievement Award sponsored by the Women's Fund, an organization based in Northern California, in 2001 (support.com website). Currently, she teaches executive management in a local university in the Bay Area. In her words, she wants to be remembered:

. . . As one who had a good balance between family and work and community. I certainly want support.com to be remembered by history. I am not vain enough to think I will be remembered by history. I want to make support.com long term sustainable.... In five years I want to start a school for young girls to make them more confident. (*International Channel* of the San Francisco Bay Area, 25 August 2001)

Basu emphasizes that the road to her successful career has not been without stresses and strains, especially on the family front:

Usually I am not at home when my daughter returns from school. If she finds me at home when she returns from school then she is surprised and asks me if everything is OK or not! Sometimes, I fly back from an out-of-town business trip just when my husband is departing for a business trip of his own. My husband hands over the baby to me as soon as I arrive at the airport gate, and then, immediately afterwards, he leaves for his own flight. There is no security, what if my flight is late, what if he has to change the timing of his flight? (*International Channel* of the San Francisco Bay Area, 25 August 2001)

It is clear that Basu has done a great deal for the progress of female empowerment—she is widely recognized for leading the way in establishing Hewlett Packard's offshore software centres in the 1980s, as well as for her entrepreneurial success in leading SupportSoft, a fledgling technology based company through various levels of public offerings to the ultimate position of a global market-leader in its field. Despite her groundbreaking professional achievements, her family commitments remain firm. In fact she does her best to make both work and home function smoothly at the same time.

Nevertheless, she still finds time for voluntary work and for example, she co-founded Maitri, a San Francisco Bay Area non-profit organization that helps South Asian victims of domestic abuse, in 1991. She currently assists in running the Anudip Foundation, a rural development organization based in India. The fact that Basu has been highly successful in her career and still been able to take time for her family and non-profit work commitments means that she is more empowered for achieving both, her devotion to family and her charity work reinforce her empowerment as a woman of substance.

Hailed as 'an emerging literary celebrity' by *Time* magazine in 2000, Chitra Banerjee Divakaruni has a dedicated fan following and is another high profile woman in the Bay Area. One often hears her interviews on National Public Radio (NPR), or reads announcements of her book readings at various bookstores in different parts of the US. Having arrived in America at the age of 19, Divakaruni completed a Masters in English Literature at Wright State University in Dayton, Ohio, and a Ph.D. in English Literature at the University of California, Berkeley, in the 1980s. Divakaruni taught at Foothill College in the San Francisco Bay Area for 20 years, and she has now retired. She devotes all her time to writing, her family, and voluntary work. She also co-founded Maitri, which she headed as President for more than a decade. A well-known poet as well as an acclaimed author of fiction, Divakaruni's poetry has been published in over 30 anthologies, and she has published 16 books of fiction. She was awarded the Santa Clara Arts Council 1994 Award for Fiction and the Wallace Alexander Gerbode Foundation 1994 Award for Poetry. She won the 1996 American Book, the Bay Area Reviewers, and the PEN Oakland Awards for Fiction for her collection of short stories, *Arranged Marriage*. Two of her novels—*The Mistress of Spices,* and *Sister of my Heart*—have been adapted into movies. Among numerous awards presented to Divakaruni in the last few years, the Women of Achievement Award sponsored by the Women's Fund of Northern California in 2001, and the South Asian Literary Association Distinguished Author Award given in 2007, are notable.

Divakaruni's popularity is not confined to the Indian community, she has a mainstream following. In an interview with her in her home in 2001, Divakaruni told me, 'I've always been received with a positive attitude by the mainstream American community. My writings have been very well received. In my readings usually half the audience is Indian, the other half is American'. Though she did not wish to discuss the effect of her public persona on domestic relations, she emphasized that home and work are equally important for her: 'For me, my career and family are equally important, I want to give time to both of them, it is an ongoing process'. Divakaruni is in many ways a traditional Hindu woman. For example, like most devout Hindus, she is vegetarian. She also takes her two young sons to Hindu scripture classes every Sunday at the local Chinmaya Mission where she also teaches Hindu scripture recitation. When we had dinner at her home, she and her mother cooked, while her husband entertained the guests and kept the children occupied.

However, in many other ways, she does not fit the picture of the traditionalist Indian immigrant woman. She devotes a lot of her time to running Maitri, and the evening we spent at her home, after feeding her guests, she had a meeting with a Bay Area techie, a young male second generation Indian immigrant, who wanted to donate some of his time and technical skills to Maitri. Placing misplaced feelings of communal loyalty above women's rights, certain conservative sections of the Indian community in the US go as far as to complain that feminists give all Indian Americans a bad name by giving undue publicity to isolated cases of domestic abuse by Indian Americans. Hence, Divakaruni can also be said to be subversive, and certainly not a traditional preserver of the status quo. Also, Divakaruni's writings about inequitable male-female relations among Indians confounds the conventional Indian immigrant tendency to cover up all the problems in the community. She explained:

I've received more criticism from Indians. This is mainly because I sometimes write about sensitive topics. Traditional people in the Indian community do not like this, they want to project Indians as a model minority. But I think that if there is a problem we should work towards solving it.

MARRIAGE, ROMANCE, AND SEXUALITY

Romantic Love

When a newly married Indian couple leaves India to come to the US, they leave behind all of their family. This is an advantage because in India, the first few years of married life are usually very difficult for an Indian bride, for she must learn the ways of her husband's household under the exacting tutelage of her mother-in-law and other female elders in the family. However, if her marriage is to a NRI (Non-Resident Indian), then she comes away with her husband to the US and the newly married couple can enjoy an initial period of uninterrupted marital bliss.

Many of the women I spoke to mentioned that though they feel guilty about leaving behind aging parents and parents-in-law in India, they enjoy the freedom from daily responsibilities it gives them, and they are fond of spending time with their husband and children rather than accompany their elders on visits to various relatives every weekend. They also take pleasure in the fact that they can make decisions without having to constantly answer to elders and other well-wishers in the extended family.

As with all other nuclear family units, the advent of children allows less time for romantic interaction between the husband and wife. Swati says, 'Ramesh and I don't need any birth control, our two children are our birth-control, the two of them keep us so busy, we have no time for each other!' Indian immigrant couples like Swati and Ramesh feel they have an especially hard time bringing up kids in the US because they are acutely aware that had they been in India, not only would *ayahs* (nannies) have been eminently affordable, but it is also likely that the couple would have received help from their parents. In the typical Indian joint family, childcare is usually shared between grandparents, parents, uncles, aunts, and domestic servants. Even nuclear families in India get regular help with childcare from the children's grandparents if the latter happen to live in the same city. Though many Indian immigrant couples bring their parents to the US to help with the care of newborn babies, most grandparents leave after six months, the maximum period allocated by the visitor visa. Thus, although the presence of children creates new bonds between the Indian immigrant husband and wife, preoccupation with children is a deterrent for romantic time spent together.

Replacement of couple time with family time was a common trend among the Indian families I studied in the San Francisco Bay Area. This is especially true of first generation Indian immigrants, who are rarely comfortable hiring middle-school or high-school teenagers as babysitters for their children. Besides, they usually do not know their predominantly non-Indian neighbours well enough to seek out babysitters from amongst the neighbourhood teenagers. Moreover, first generation Indian immigrant parents rarely encourage their US-born and raised teenagers to earn money through babysitting for Indian parents believe that their children, even teenagers, should devote all of their time to studying, or sports, or music and dance lessons, rather than starting to earn money at such a young age. Thus it is difficult for first generation Indian immigrant parents to procure babysitters from amongst the teenage offspring of their Indian friends. First generation immigrant parents may leave their children at a daycare centre so that they can go to work, but they will rarely leave their children with a babysitter to enjoy an evening in each other's company. All social activities in the Indian immigrant community include children. Children are taken to lunch and dinner parties, they accompany their parents to Indian music concerts and dance performances, restaurant meals are family events, and Indian-American offspring go to see not just children's movies but also many other Indian movies with their parents.

Though the achievements of the working women often enable them to earn their husband's respect, full-time work naturally reduces the time they can spend with their families, and consequently, with their husbands. In fact, in most of the Indian immigrant families I interviewed and observed, the woman leaves for work very early in the morning while her husband drops the children to school or daycare and then goes to work himself. The wife often leaves work as early as 4 p.m. so that she can pick up the children from school or daycare, bring them home, feed them, and supervise their bath time. She then cooks dinner, oversees the children's homework, and packs the lunch boxes for the next day. The husband often comes home from work as late as 8 p.m. or 8.30 p.m., by which time the family has dinner together, and the children to go to bed. The majority of the Indian immigrant working women I spoke to described slight variations of the above as their typical daily routine. We can see that in a typical weekday, barely an hour is spent by the whole family together, and the couple hardly gets to spend more than an hour or two exclusively in each other's company.

Female Image

The traditional Indian norm, as well as ideal, is that a married woman, and especially a mother, devotes all her time to household and childcare duties; she should not waste time on 'dressing up'. In conservative Indian circles, the prevailing morality dictates that all men and women must cease to 'dress up' when they enter middle age or when their children enter their adolescence. This signifies the end of the Indian middle-aged mother's sexual identity. At this stage of life, the women aim to derive power not from their physical charm, but from their senior status, and their supervisory authority over their children and other junior family members. Although middle class Indian men wear Western clothes far more often than Indian clothes, traditionally, when they dress in Indian attire, older men wear white and light pastel colours. Older Indian women hardly ever diet or exercise for the sake of beauty or physical fitness, consequently it is difficult for them to maintain their figures. They are often expected to wear drab colours, and lightly coloured saris with coloured borders tend to be favoured by the matriarch even while her unmarried daughters and newly married daughters-in-law wear a riot of brightly coloured attractive fabrics with gold or silver thread embroidery. Widows are required to forsake all jewellery and to wear white saris.

The American emphasis on youth and looking good stresses an ideal that is contrary to the Indian emphasis on moving beyond physical attractiveness towards more spiritual objectives once one enters middle age. The American sartorial ideal holds that everyone, irrespective of their age, should make an effort to look good. Self-care is emphasized and beauty is showcased because attractiveness continues to be part of the individual's charisma even after the reproductive stage is over. Indian American immigrant women, and men too, are caught between these two contrary ideals.

Most Indian immigrants to the US do make concessions to the American emphasis on always looking at least presentable. Most middle class Indian immigrants try to take care of their bodies, many exercise and work out regularly, they dye their hair when it starts turning white, undergo various types of other beauty treatments, and they buy what they hope are current American fashions in departmental store sales. When they visit India, NRIs buy suitcases full of youngish, that is, colourful, and richly patterned, shirts, skirts, jeans, salwar kameezes, saris, and sari-blouses. The Americanization of the immigrant's viewpoint is evident from Kalyani's comment:

In India, once the offspring reach marriageable age, their mothers begin to dress in drab clothes. Women over thirty-five stop wearing bright colours. They stick to boring light pastel colours. They don't 'dress up' any more. I wonder why they purposely make themselves look ugly!

However, speaking from the opposite viewpoint, while on a visit to the Bay Area, a visitor from India wryly observed that, 'America is the place of *chirobosonto* (everlasting spring). Even older women in the Indian immigrant community in the US dress so gaudily, they wear such brightly coloured saris!'

Yet, despite their efforts to look young and fashionable, deep-seated insecurities exist among many Indian immigrant women who are concerned about their attractiveness, particularly in the American milieu. As well as appearance, behaviour is also a source of confusion and insecurity. The research conducted for this study reveals that many first generation Indian immigrant women are confused about how they should behave: should they be 'good' Indian women or liberated and progressive Americans?

COMPARISON OF WORKING AND NON-WORKING WOMEN

Degrees of Empowerment

In my research in the Indian immigrant community in the San Francisco Bay Area, I found that as far as decision-making power at home is concerned, working women are at an advantage when compared to non-working women. Indian immigrant working women are more empowered than housewives in the community.

Non-working women in the Indian immigrant community seem to have lives rather similar to those of White American housewives a few decades ago, as described by Betty Friedan in her book *The Feminine Mystique* (1963). Friedan discussed the unsatisfactory stay-at-home lives of White middle class American women in the early 1960s. At that time, most middle class White women were not employed and Friedan called for 'a new life plan' for such women. She advocated that women escape from the 'housewife trap' and attempt to construct a new, more purposeful self. Friedan insisted that the transition to a new self would not be difficult for (White) American women for:

Once she begins to see through the delusions of the feminine mystique—and realizes that neither her husband nor her children, nor the things in her house, nor sex, nor being like all other women, can give her a self—she often finds the solution much easier than she had anticipated. (1963: 339)

Friedan insisted that women have not only the right to love, children, and home, rights that 'have defined femininity in the past', but also the right to 'work towards a greater purpose that shapes the future' (1964: 338). In the last four decades, American women have won themselves many, if not most, of the changes sought by Friedan. However, as Hochschild has shown, this transformation in the role of women has created a double workload for working women.

Housework and Childcare

Arlie Hochschild points out that most families in contemporary America are double job families, and that most women in this situation complete their day job, 'the first shift', only to return home to the 'second shift' of housework and childcare. Currently, 58.6 per cent of American women over the age of 16 work, and they form 47 per cent of the American workforce (2010 US Census). Despite the post-1960s myth of male-female equality at home, Hochschild found that only 20 per cent of men in the two-job families she studied shared housework and childcare equally with their wives (1989: 8). Household work continues to be divided according to gender, with women performing the vast majority of repetitive indoor housework tasks and men performing occasional outdoor tasks (Coltrane 2000). A recent study conducted in 2011 found that 84 per cent of American women and 67 per cent of American men conducted household activities such as housework, preparation of food, gardening, or other home management chores in the course of an average day ('American Time Use Summary' 2011).

Due to various reasons including the ideological and legal gains of the women's liberation movement, pervasive unemployment caused by the lingering recession, continuing inflation, the recent decline of (traditionally male) manufacturing and construction jobs due to offshoring and increased automation, and the present proliferation of female service sector jobs, more American women have now joined the labour force that ever before. However, there is a substantial wage gap between men and women, and at the time Hochschild did her study 46 per cent of working women in America earned less than $10,000 a year (1989: 25), and the average American wife earned only one-third of her husband's earnings (ibid.: 219). Currently, the American female-to-male earning ration is 0.77, that is, women earn 77 cents on the dollar (2010 US Census).

Divorce is also an ever-present possibility for married American couples. The divorce rate is very high in America and approximately half of those who marry today are likely to divorce their spouse. In terms of personal finance, divorce can often hurt women more than men. Quoting Lenora Weitzman, Hochschild states that 'in the first year after divorce women experience a 73 per cent loss in the standard of living, whereas men experience a 42 per cent gain' (1989: 249). Few men pay child support: only 20 per cent of the fathers asked by the court to pay child support do so regularly, 15 per cent only pay irregularly, and the rest do not pay any child support at all (ibid.). Due to all these factors, despite their new commitments as full-time participants in the labour force, numerous American women hesitate to press their husbands when the latter resist a renegotiation of the traditional (inequitable) understanding that the woman will perform almost all of the housework and childcare.

The two paragraphs above outline some characteristics of the host society in the US that receives the Indian immigrant women. The American media often writes about 'dead beat' dads, that is, non-custodial parents who do not make child-support payments to their former wives. However, there is little data on this issue. A more recent study on the lines of Hochschild's is not available but there is little reason to believe that a redistribution of the 'costs' of divorce in favour of women has taken place. Fundamentally, divorce brings about a fall of real income or the standard of living for women. However, the frequency of divorce and what it costs to women in the mainstream American population is of little consequence to the Indian immigrant women because interviews with my subjects indicate that the frequency of divorce is insignificant among Indian immigrants. On the other hand, the macro-factors in the mainstream do matter, for example, the wage gap between men and women, or the threat of impoverishment as a deterrent to contemplating divorce.

The research conducted in this study has shown that the pattern of sharing work at home is a clear indicator of the woman's status at home. I found that immigrant women who work full-time get a significant amount of help with household chores and childcare from their husbands. When the woman is the principal earner then the husband tends to take on equal household and childcare responsibilities. I found that working Indian immigrant women also employ a significant amount of domestic help: Hispanic cleaning ladies and South Asian ayahs and cooks were commonly employed by my working subjects. The easy availability of South Asian services in the San Francisco Bay Area contributed to the trend of outsourcing childcare, housework, cooking, and Indian cultural training.

Megha, the associate professor in a San Francisco Bay Area university mentioned previously, said of her husband:

The wonderful thing about Prakash having left home when he was young is that he was used to looking after himself and the house. . . . At this point we fight about the cleanliness of the house certainly, but Prakash does 60 per cent of the cooking, I do 40 per cent of the cooking, I do more of the cleaning.

When the husband is also very busy with his career then professional Indian immigrant women do not hesitate to avail themselves of hired help and daycare facilities for children. Dr Urmila Sarkar, a physician, explains that she placed her son in daycare as soon as she had weaned him from the breast. 'I placed him in daycare when he was almost three months old. It was a home daycare, a nice family. I mean I couldn't have done it without them. I mean my husband has always been busy and stuff like that. It was a Hungarian family here in Fremont.'

In keeping with Hochschild's findings, my research showed that full-time principal-earners such as Megha, Smita, and Urmila, tend to be happy in their marriages for their husbands actively share work at home. Also in keeping with Hochschild's theories, I found that many Indian immigrant housewives, part-time working women, and full-time working women who are not principal earners are discontented in their marriages because their husbands refuse to help with chores at home. Karabi, a pregnant housewife says, 'Sometimes I really don't feel like cooking, pregnancy has drained me of all my energy, and I also get awful back-pains. But my husband refuses to cook a single dish. So I spend about two hours every morning cooking.'

Similarly, Lakshmi, a full-time senior research scientist in a private pharmaceutical company says:

I am an Indian woman, my family will come first. Everyone assumes that among Indians the woman will be in charge or running the home and taking care of the family. My son says, [though] he is only eight years old, 'I am glad I'm not a woman'.

In the same way, Charulata, a full-time product manager at Delphi Technology, is unhappy with the unequal division of household chores in her home, but she blames herself for allowing her husband to get away with doing minimal household work, 'Training is a big thing. As women, we ourselves tend to give in to our men without a struggle.'

On the whole, though most of the women spoken to were well aware that they did far more work at home than their husbands, they accepted it.

Haleh Afshar writes that in general, due to their greater social power developing world men have been able to control female sexuality, enjoy the fruits of female labour both outside and inside the home, in terms of family, marriage, and the household. Afshar points out that 'the ideology of marital domesticity confines women to the role of dependent and inferior bearers of labour' (1985: xiv). This observation, made more than two decades ago, applies to fewer women today; however remnants of those inequitable traditions possibly persist in the minds of many immigrant women who resigned themselves to the single-handed juggling of household work along with full-time jobs rather than resist the long-established domestic balance of labour. As Rita Banerji has recently shown in her work, the sexual and gender hierarchy in India remains acutely skewed against women, and their well-being is still continually threatened by the cultural refusal to recognize female rights (2009).

Access to Household and Financial Resources

Hillary Standing argues that access to family resources is one of the prime indicators of status within the family. Wage earning women have better negotiating power than non-salaried women as far as access to family resources is concerned. Standing suggests that we can estimate the impact of wage earning on women's situation within the family by examining their access to family resources, 'defining resources as in a broad way to encompass education, health, different forms of property such as those accruing through inheritance or marriage settlement, cash incomes, savings and so on'. Standing suggests that we should 'try to determine whether any change occurs either in the amount or the terms of access when a woman enters wage employment' (1985: 233). Standing's study of the resources in the urban Bengali household was conducted almost 30 years ago, but the methodological point she made, looking beyond distribution of money and property to other resources like education, remains very useful.

Education and specialized training in their respective fields were commonly mentioned resources that the women I interviewed wanted access to. However, not many managed to convince their husbands to sponsor their education. Vijaylakshmi, a housewife, says:

I did some classes last year in computer languages. Since then, for one whole year Vikram has been stalling, refusing to allow me to enroll for classes. He says he is so overburdened with his work that he has no time to babysit Aryan or help me with my assignments.

On the other hand, a few of my interviewees were, in fact, fortunate enough to have supportive husbands. Ankita explains, 'There is no question, I could not have completed my degree without my husband's help at every step!' Charulata's husband moved to his wife's university town so that she could complete her studies. Kanchana obtained her husband's permission to enrol in an MBA programme in a university located hundreds of miles away. Though it was difficult to set up a temporary home so far away from her husband, she was able to visit him over the weekends. She completed the degree and returned home to the Bay Area within two years.

Motivation for Desire to Work

My research has shown that it is not just access to household resources, financial freedom, and education, but the ability to work outside the home in paid employment that is also highly coveted by Indian immigrant women. Unfortunately, those Indian immigrant women who have low-paying jobs often struggle to obtain their husband's support for their decision to hold salaried positions. Pramiti explains that her husband did not want her to go to work because he thought the paltry salary she earned was not worth the disruption her going to work caused in their household. However, she continues to work because it allows her to make use of her education in science. Moreover, though limited, her salary enables her to go shopping for certain items she wants for herself or her family without feeling guilty for indulging in frivolous spending. And she is hopeful that her current job might lead to a better employment position, one whose salary will make a significant contribution to the family. Another interviewee, Paulomi explains that she loves her home, but she does not want to be confined to her home, 'I work mainly for freedom, just to get out of the house—I feel good when I get out of the house and get involved in a work related project—it liberates me from the four walls of my home'. Lastly, Ankita says she works in order to maintain her own separate identity, her own area of expertise where she can try to excel, 'My work gives me a chance to express myself and focus on projects I enjoy and am proficient in'. The hope is that the prestige generated from her work might be converted into some privileges for her family.

In addition to the points mentioned above, employment affords the opportunity to make new friends, especially among native-born Americans. Working women get a chance to make friends other than their husband's friends' wives. Kalyani says, 'I told Arjun I'm tired of trying to be your friends' wives' friend, they are too scheming and gossipy. Why should I not make friends with the White girls I work with?' Kalyani has invited her White friends from the preschool she teaches in on numerous occasions, and she and her family enjoy socializing with them.

Motivations for the Desire to Stay at Home

Many Indian immigrant non-working mothers claim that they opt to stay at home full-time so that they can devote all of their time and energy to raising their children in a proper manner. They say that since their children are being raised in an alien environment, it is the parents' duty, and especially the mother's responsibility, to teach Indian culture to the new generation of Indian Americans. This attitude seems somewhat problematic because living in the San Francisco Bay Area, it is easy for Indian immigrant working mothers to arrange for Indian childcare due to the high immigrant population in the Bay Area, of which 119,854 are Indians (2010 US Census).

Aihwa Ong tells us that Chinese transnational immigrant families will set up home, albeit a transitory home, in foreign lands for the sake of capital accumulation. Cultural capital is not given up, for the immigrant family keeps its roots in the nation of origin, and sets up ethnic cultural networks in the land of settlement. The ultimate ambition is to convert economic capital into prestige capital in the new land as well as in the country of birth (1999). Indian immigrants follow this model, and Indian immigrant working women engage in economic production as well as in cultural and biological reproduction in order to attain the goal of prestige accumulation for their family and ethnic group.

Due to an unprecedented influx of immigrants into the US, and because of the acceleration of transnational discourses in mass print and electronic media, we now live in a post-national world of diasporic public spheres in which the state must construct a society around diasporic diversity (Appadurai 1996). Easily-accessible personal media such as phone, home video, and electronic mail combine with the ease of long distance travel to facilitate the continuation of friendships between individuals separated by thousands of geographical miles (Hannerz 2002).

As previously discussed, the ability to indulge in diasporic cultural activities to the fullest extent in America, and specifically in the San Francisco Bay Area, allows working Indian immigrant wives to continue cultural reproduction through locally available Indian resources. These include Indian childcare centres, caterers, movies, TV shows, groceries for their Indian nannies to cook for the children, prayers, dances, and songs taught by local Indian instructors, and frequent visits from their relatives in India.

Thus, due to the availability of Indian cultural trainers within the Bay Area, Indian immigrant working wives and mothers have no trouble outsourcing the enculturation of their children to Indian nannies, music and dance teachers, and cooks should they so desire. Hence, they can continue economic production along with biological and cultural reproduction. Also, family from India can be flown in to the US to provide further, and perhaps more authentic, Indianization and enculturation. The easy availability of Indian mass and personal media facilitate the passing on of traditional Indian culture to second generation Indian Americans even in the absence of employed Indian immigrant mothers from their homes during working hours.

The question of how authentic or current the culture passed on to the immigrant children is will now be addressed. Sucheta Mazumdar insists that what is passed on is outdated, and even worse, usually a means used by the first generation to restrict the freedom of the second generation (1996). Espiritu has also shown in her work among the Filipinos of San Diego that what passes for native ethnic culture is often deployed by the parental generation to limit the individuation of teenage and young adult immigrant offspring (2003). I personally observed many instances in which elders in the Indian immigrant families imposed behavioural strictures that are certainly outdated, if not inauthentic, for the purpose of keeping the younger generation in check. For example, Pia, who came recently from India with her husband and two children says:

We grew up with family: not just parents, and brothers, and sisters, but also cousins, grandparents and other relatives constantly around us. But our children who grow up here do not have that. So it is up to the parents to look after them. . . . Parents are responsible for their children's success. My husband wants me to devote all my time to my children so that they get all the attention they need.

Pia went on to say that she wants her daughter Sheela to be 'simple, like the girls growing up in India', and she does not want Sheela to pay too much attention to her appearance. Hence, she discourages her from removing the hair from her arms and legs even though high-school-going girls of Sheela's age commonly use hair-removing lotions, shaving creams, or waxing paper in India for that very purpose. In fact that is the current norm in urban middle class India. In another instance of outdated norms, Bimala criticized the revealing style of dress among her son's female classmates in middle-school, and said she really doesn't want her son to mix with those girls. However, the truth of the matter is that nowadays Indian middle-school girls in cosmopolitan cities also wear short skirts to school.

Comparison

Most of the non-working Indian immigrant women I spoke to were insistent that because they were able to spend more time with their children, they succeeded in transmitting more Indian habits and values, and hence were able to counteract the unsuitable influences of American culture on their children.

All the Indian immigrant housewives I spoke to emphasized that spending maximum time with their children was 'the best thing they could do for their kids'. Leela says:

My first child grew up in daycare. When my second was born, I told my husband that I wanted to stay at home with the new baby for a few years, and I have done that, now she is two years old. You know, the more time you spend with your children the more attached you grow to them.

Despite this, working Indian immigrant women said that their children are no less emotionally attached to them than the children of non-working Indian immigrant mothers. Due to the after-school hours spent in daycare, such children are less proficient in Indian languages than the children of stay-at-home Indian immigrant mothers, they are not very fond of Indian food, etc. Indian immigrant working mothers do not see this as a problem for they argue that there is no point fighting a losing battle to Indianize their children when they will spend their entire lives in the US anyway. Aware that their children will only spend a few weeks a year in India, they do not feel there is any need to make the effort to inculcate Indian habits. Furthermore, working Indian American women argue that in case some Indian immigrant parents feels the urge to familiarize the younger generation with a taste of Indian culture and values then they can always outsource enculturation since there are many individuals and organizations that specialize in this service in the Bay Area. In any case, it makes little sense to give up one's career for the sake of teaching Indian culture to one's children.

On the other hand, as indicated earlier, Indian immigrant non-working women claimed that they were doing the best thing possible for their children by staying at home full-time and devoting all their energies to child rearing. Indian diasporic women are burdened with something more than the common American phenomenon of the 'Mommy Mystique', a phrase coined by Judith Warner. The 'Mommy Mystique' is:

> . . . an almost religious adherence to ideas about child rearing, about marriage and sex-roles and society that supports the status quo even as mothers denounce it, even as children complain about it, even as 'the experts' warn that our way of doing things is stressing children to the core. (2005: 32)

Besides being weighed down by the conservative 'Mommy Mystique', immigrant mothers shoulder the responsibility of acculturating their children in their native culture as well. Non-working immigrant mothers claim to be better at both childcare and cultural training than their working counterparts, but this is not the case. Indian immigrant working mothers have enough childcare and ethno-cultural resources in the Bay Area to outsource significant portions of both child rearing and enculturation to professionals.

SELF/IDENTITY AT HOME, IN THE FAMILY, AND IN THE COMMUNITY

Claude Steele argues that all comprehensive models of the self contain a self-system that functions to 'sustain phenomenal experience images of the self, past, present, and future as having adaptive and moral adequacy, as being competent, good, stable, integrated, capable of choice and control, and so forth' (1988: 289). Steele's psychological theories are significant because they show that the goal of the self-system is to 'maintain global conceptions of self-adequacy' (ibid.: 287). Steele found that people eliminate the effects of specific self-threats by 'affirming central, valued, aspects of the self' (ibid.: 289).

As has also been discussed in Chapter II, participation in the American workforce encourages progress in self and identity formation. However, at the same time, increased exposure to non-Indians, that is to Americans of various types, hastens the realization that female Asian Indian immigrants are unlikely to be accepted by mainstream Americans. The realization that they will never be accepted by mainstream Americans threatens the self-esteem of Indian immigrant working women. The self-affirmation theory (Steele 1988), helps us to comprehend how individuals cope with self-threats. This theory states that all human beings are highly motivated to protect and maintain a global sense of self integrity. Hence, people respond to threatening information defensively and they downplay, diminish, or disregard threatening information. As people want to maintain their global sense of self-integrity, they attempt to restore self-integrity by drawing on alternative sources that are not related to the threat. Hence Indian immigrant women cope with the disquieting realization that they will never be accepted by the mainstream in their host nation by affirming other domains.

Indian immigrant working women attempt to reduce the pressure of self-threatening thoughts about regarding the impossibility of being accepted as an American by Americans, by conjuring up self-affirming thoughts about, for example, their career highlights, their financial security, their artistic achievements, the achievements of their children, their popularity within the Indian immigrant community, and the respect and affection they receive as successful NRIs when they visit their family in India. This psychological adaptation aids the perception of global self-integrity.

One common source of self-affirming thoughts revolves around the acquisition of possessions in America. This may be the reason why Indian Americans are so competitive about acquiring the newest electrical gadgets and electronic equipment as soon as they are released in the market. Women compete with each other to buy the trendiest clothes, shoes, and jewellery for themselves and their families. The ownership of real estate, expensive cars, and the regular purchase of exotic vacation packages all add up to the achievement of an adequately affluent lifestyle that provides the self-afffirmation necessary to cope with the self-threat of lack of acceptance by the American mainstream.

Another source of self-affirming thoughts relate to the gift-giving capacities of the women. Giving expensive gifts to extended family members in India is a major method of procuring prestige in the extended family. When Kalyani goes to India on her annual vacation, she loads her suitcases with US-made perfumes, colognes, soaps, shampoos, fine china, sweaters, shirts, purses, and wallets. She also buys a few small electronic items such as cameras and watches to give to friends and relatives in India. Lastly, she takes a few gold guineas to give to especially close relatives. Now that the Indian market has been liberalized and foreign goods are freely sold there, all of these items are likely to be currently available, but it is convenient to buy them before leaving the US. The women like to gift their friends and relatives lavishly in order to give the impression that despite India's recent economic upturn, they have a higher standard of living in the US than their contemporaries in India.

Another form of self-affirmation is through one's children. Many Indian American mothers try to live through their children. They vie with each other to have their children win the highest academic, sports, and artistic honours. They also train their children in the same, or similar, cultural skills as their own, and expect the children to excel in them. Cultural programmes held during religious festivals such as Diwali, or Indian shows organized during Indian National holidays such as Indian Independence Day, provide venues to showcase the children's talents in music and dance.

Yet another form of self-affirmation is to become active in Indian cultural activities such as music, dance, and theatre oneself. Active participation in one's religious festivals, whether Hindu, Sikh, Jain, Islamic, or Buddhist, is also a great source of self-satisfaction. Social gatherings provide a forum to get-together with other Indian Americans and form a mutually supportive community.

The continuity achieved by the methods described above helps the women affirm their own identity. Such psychological mechanisms aid in the process of what Steele calls 'adaptive and moral adequacy' in that it helps to make the women feel competent, good, stable, integrated, and capable of choice and control (1988: 289). Paradoxically, affirming the separate selves can help to soothe the individual even if that affirmation heightens the contradiction between the 'American self' and the 'Indian self'.

It is important to evaluate the positive as well as negative effects of joining the American workforce as far as Indian women in the US are concerned. There are numerous positive psychological effects of joining the American workforce. For example, in comparison to the stay-at-home Indian immigrant wives and mothers, career-oriented Indian American woman have more opportunity to acculturate into the mainstream of American culture. This in turn can increase their level of comfort in the newly-adopted nation.

Another important development in the independent identity formation of Indian immigrant career women is that with the emphasis on male-female equality in the workplace, women feel more empowered. This emphasis may be superficial, but nevertheless, even the rhetoric, if not the unfailing practice, of workplace gender equity has a significant psychological impact.

However, as discussed before, the conflicting demands of the roles of the career-oriented woman in the American workforce on one hand, and that of the traditional Indian housewife on the other, create considerable dissonance in the psyche of the Asian Indian immigrant woman. The women perceive that they will not be accepted by the mainstream for they will always be viewed as foreigners. This essentialization pushes the women to reassert their Indian identity with renewed vigour. At the same time, the women fear that exaggerated displays of Indianness in the workplace will destroy what little chances they have of acceptance. Hence, home is the location for the reversion to Indian habits and the re-construction of the Indian self. Unfourtunately, the return to Indianness at home means a return to the inequitable patriarchal relations that characterize the traditional Indian family. Unlike many of their American counterparts, as Indian wives, they are expected to take care of childcare and housework with little help from the male members of the family. This inequity at home is difficult to accept for Indian immigrant women who, learning from the gender equity of the workplace, aspire to be treated equally. These contradictory demands create a self which is conflicted and dissonance-ridden.

CONCLUSION

I have interviewed Indian working women and non-working women in the Bay Area, and working women in India. Despite a steady process of Americanization over time, the Indian transnational community in the US is extremely concerned about the transmission of Indian culture to the next generation. Women are usually held responsible for this process. Non-working Indian immigrant women personally acculturate their children, but working Indian immigrant mothers are no less active in exposing their children to Indian culture. Despite the time spent away from home because of work commitments, Indian immigrant working women in the Bay Area create an Indian ambience at home by availing themselves of the readily available services of immigrant Indian nannies, cultural teachers, clothes retailers, food caterers, grocers, and media dispensers. Though Indian diasporic working mothers arrange for their children to learn Indian culture while they are at work, Indian immigrant non-working women emphasize that their constant presence at home is necessary for the proper enculturation of their children in so-called Indian traditions. They are critical of women who have stepped out of domestic boundaries in order to contribute monetarily to the well-being of the family. Indian immigrant parents as well as diasporic community leaders claim that their cultural productions are replicas of their counterparts in India. Thus when we discuss cultural deployment in transnational families/communities, the debate must shift to an assessment of whether the culture that is passed on is authentic, updated, and reflective of the diversity of the lived culture in the nation of origin.

Working outside the home in paid employment brings women appreciation for their contribution to the household income, and it gives them agency and access to household resources. Non-working transnational women rationalize their relative lack of ability to financially assist their family, and their lesser independence and access to household resources by stressing their success in the recreation of Indian culture at home and in community gatherings.

The selves of immigrant working women are Americanized by their functioning in the American workplace, even though the multicultural workforce and the significant presence of Indians in the local population, and especially in the Silicon Valley, diminishes the mainstreaming effect of employment. Along with Americanization comes the realization that Indian immigrant women, especially first generation entrants, are likely to continue to be viewed primarily as Indians by native-born Americans. This essentialization causes a threat to the self to which the usual response is varied attempts at self-affirmation in different areas of one's life.

CHAPTER IV

The Construction of the Self

INTRODUCTION

INDIAN IMMIGRANTS make many strategic adjustments to improve their position in the country of settlement. Whether they swear singular allegiance to the US, jettisoning the language, food, clothes, and habits of their country of origin in order to 'blend in', or whether they emphasize the deterritorialized plurality of their global selves, they are all struggling to come to terms with the unfamiliar customs of the new country. Equally, they are faced with the cultural, social, and economic anxieties of being a racial and ethnic minority in their adopted country. As they themselves say, they want the best of both worlds: American material comforts and freedom, alongside Indian culture and community. This chapter will discuss whether the subjects succeeded in this endeavour, or whether they ended up caught between the difficulties of maintaining two or more opposite and contrasting identities.

THE SELF-CONCEPTION OF ASIAN INDIAN PROFESSIONAL WORKING WOMEN IN THE BAY AREA

In terms of the concepts of self and identity and the interplay between the Indian self/identity and the American self/identity, professional Indian working women in the Bay Area can be broadly divided into three separate categories:

(i) Recent entrants (residence and work experience of one to two years in the US).
(ii) Medium duration (residence and work experience of two to ten years in the US).
(iii) Long duration (residence and work experience of more than ten years in the US).

In the following sections, the self and identity in these three categories will also be compared with that of Indian non-working women resident in the US.

I. RECENT ENTRANTS

Yearning to Come to America

Imperialism, neo-colonialism, and economic expansion by the West disrupted non-Western economies and social systems, and spurred an unprecedented steady stream of migration to the West since the 1960s (Bonacich and Cheng 1984; Ong, Bonacich and Cheng 1994). Post-colonial identification with Western colonial powers, and American commodified global mass culture of the late capitalist era have served to familiarize Indians, especially educated middle and upper class Indians, with Western culture as a whole, and British and American culture in particular (Bhabha 1994; Hall 1997).

The Indian professional working women that I observed, interacted with, and interviewed in the San Francisco Bay Area for this study, had been vastly affected by post-colonial and neo-colonial fascination with the West even before they had departed from India. They were subconsciously part of the the human legacy of British colonial history, and the ideological by-products of current American globalization of the economy and world culture and rapidly becoming part of the international circuits of global immigration.

Nayana's grandfather studied in Britain and he was a senior officer in the British colonial administration in India. Nayana's father also did his graduate studies in UK, and so they were both 'Brown sahibs'. Highly educated post-colonial natives such as these tended to identify more with their former colonizers than with the masses in their own nation. Hence, they would rather indulge in 'mimicry of colonial masculinity and mimesis' than embrace new Indian nationalist culture (Bhabha 1994: 168). The colonial natives in the imperial periphery identified with their British rulers to such an extent that when colonial rule ended, some of them followed the British to Britain: 'The very moment when finally Britain convinced itself it had to decolonize, it had to get rid of them, we all came back home. As they hauled down the flag, we got on the banana boat and sailed right into London' (Hall 1997: 24). In any case, when Nayana's father returned to India after his education in Britain, he brought a British accent and English tastes with him.

Nayana herself grew up in upper middle class India. Like other elite Indians of her generation, she was raised on a post-colonial diet of 'classic' British literature, as well as on American movies, music, cars, food, and clothing fashions. Her childhood home was filled with old British memorabilia and new American imported goods.

Unlike her parents and grandfather, Nayana was part of the generation attracted not by post-colonial yearnings for 'back home', that is, England, but by American global mass culture. Western, specifically American popular culture, seduces people over the world to set up home in the US, and images, visuals, and graphic arts from the US reconstitute popular life all over the world. American television, film, and mass advertising shape entertainment and leisure across linguistic frontiers. Satellite television is the prime example of a form of mass communication that cannot be limited by national boundaries, but which originates from and is controlled by developed world nations and cultures (Hall 1997). Global mass culture 'remains centred in the West', and it is powered by Western technology, capital, and representations of Western societies. Secondly, global mass culture is a 'homogeneous form of cultural representation, enormously absorptive of things, as it were, but the homogenization is never absolutely complete, and it does not work for completeness'. It accepts that there will be differences 'within the framework of what is essentially an American conception of the world' (ibid.: 28). Indian immigrants are drawn to the US by its leadership in technology, capital, and global mass culture.

Gurcharan Das also writes of Indians learning American ways without leaving their own homeland when he points out how the communications revolution of the 1990s had drawn the world into Indian homes for the first time, and how this led Indians to discover how far India lagged behind other nations of the world, specially advanced nations. The average Indian welcomed the changes brought about in India's new age of liberalization because television, cable, and the Internet heightened his/her awareness of the new opportunities that would become available when the Indian economy opened up to the rest of the world (Das 2002). However, having become aware of how much work India had to do before it could liberate itself from the licence Raj and transform itself into a free-market economy, many Indian youths decided to move to the US, the preeminent economy of the world, at once. Higher education in the US was the preferred means of entry to the US. Most Indian students who completed their Ph.Ds. in the US obtained employment here after completion of their degrees and stayed on here.

Nayana came to the US to do a Ph.D. in physics, and having been able to find a job here right after finishing her degree, she has stayed on. She says, 'When I graduated from school, the expectation was that I would study in England, as my parents and grandfather had done, but I wanted to come to the US. So I did.' And she has made the US her home.

THE SHOCK OF ARRIVAL

Colonial memories, as well as the new American cultural global outreach, give non-Westerners the impression that they are familiar with Western culture. It is of course impossible to know the West until one actually lives in it. For Indians, though they are enamoured with the West, all internal psychic development has taken place in an Indian social context. What G.H. Mead called the inner 'I', remains intrinsically Indian. It may be a post-colonial 'I', it may be submerged in dominant American mass culture, but nevertheless, it is an Indian 'I', as will be discussed later in this chapter. For example, inter-gender interaction is typically Indian, not Western. Without essentializing Indian and American social behaviour, it is possible to argue that in comparison to their American counterparts, Indian men and women avoid social interaction with each other while in the public gaze. Remarking on the difference between Indian and American female attitudes to men, Amitrajit (a male informant) said American women are 'friendly' but Indian women are 'stand-offish' (in both India as well as the US). One reason for this is that in the Indian workplace, men and women can socialize with each other only at the risk of triggering rumours of the woman having 'lost her decency'.

Jishnu (a male informant) grew up in a large cosmopolitan city. He went to a co-educational school, but in India he was seldom exposed to the semi-clothed female body. This is obvious in the following anecdote he related about his first year in the US. Jishnu says:

In my first year in the US, when I was an undergraduate student, in our dorm the water pipe in the boys' restroom burst. So we boys had to use the girls' restroom for a few days. The girls would come out of the shower stalls and go to their rooms in their bath towels, right in front of us boys. Fresh from India, I was totally amazed by this behaviour, I couldn't believe my eyes.

Indian men in America find out that they must take the open and friendly manner of American women in their stride. At the same time, they see that rules forbidding sexual harassment in the workplace are stringently enforced in the US. In 2003, the Indian Chief Executive Officer of the American branch of Infosys, an Indian software company, was removed from his post following charges of sexual harassment brought against him by his former secretary, an American woman. In contrast, once they arrive in the US, Indian women find that they must not be 'shy', and they learn that in the US, women and men are expected to interact in a free and friendly manner.

Let alone the nuances of inter-gender behaviour, just day-to-day functioning in America may turn out to be a challenge for 'Fresh Off the Boat' (FOB) immigrants. Ankita says:

When I arrived in the US, I knew very good 'Indian convent-school English', but I had difficulty making myself understood because my accent was so different from the American accent. Also, I felt uncomfortable driving on the 'wrong' side of the road. I had to figure out the values of dollars, dimes, cents and pennies, and someone had to explain how to work the coin-operated laundry machine before I could wash my own clothes!

FOB Indians are the subject of much immigrant humour. There is a popular joke about an FOB Indian vegetarian who is very hungry. He orders a cheese burger at McDonald's expecting to find only cheese in it, and he is outraged to find a meat burger between the buns. This story is often told at Indian immigrant parties and get-togethers and though humourous, is a good indicator of how alien the culture can be to newcomers.

In general, American global, cultural, and economic clout attract people from all over the world. They want to enjoy the 'good life' perceived to be found in the US, but ironically, once they arrive, visitors, sojourners, and immigrants alike all experience the shock of arrival. In comparison to India, social behaviour, public/private interactions, and role expectations are very different in the US.

Ankita explains:

In India, I was considered fair [of complexion], my height was about the Indian average height. I could speak good English, I wore fashionable locally-made clothes. But here, surrounded by pink complexions, and deodorized Americans, I suddenly felt very dark, short and bad smelling. My clothes, even the skirts, shirts and pants I had bought for myself in India, seemed strange, ill-fitting, and completely out of fashion in the US. In shops, sales people, though trained to be polite, were reluctant to serve me, even suspicious that I might be a shoplifter. Whereas in India, the sales people would sense my upper/middle class status at once, and hasten help me, saying *Namaste Madam, aap kya lenge*? [Madame, how may I help you?].

Indians undergo racinization (to be identified primarily by racial and ethnic characteristics and culture of origin) when they come to the US. Their class position is lost upon exit from India and arrival in the US. They are no longer middle or upper class English-speaking privileged youth, but rather, they become economically disadvantaged brown students or entry level workers who are repeatedly asked to prove the legality of their presence in the US. This is what Rosemary George has referred to as the fall from 'expatriate aristocrat to immigrant nobody' (1997).

Women who have not lived or been in the American workforce for long, are discomfited by demands to shuttle back and forth between their desire to fit in with Americans and their identity as an Indian. They are extremely confident of their technical knowledge in their field of expertise, but they are unsure about how to interact with Americans in social situations.

For example, Niharika, a software engineer at Mallory-Powers has been in the US for only three years. She is confident about work-related interactions with her colleagues, but she admits that she is at a loss about how to make small talk with her non-Indian mainstream American colleagues, 'I think professionally they [Americans] perceive us like most Americans', and, 'Professionally they [Americans] treat you absolutely as equals, there is nothing like "You come from India, you are different". There is no difference whatsoever professionally.' However, she feels that it is not easy to interact with most Americans at a social level:

So I don't think they know much about Indians and Indian women and all that. I was taking a course in University of California, Santa Cruz Extension College. So there I picked up one American, I mean I became friends with one American guy. He was very interested in India; so it is easy to talk to such people.

Mrigakshi is a software tester at Sabine Information Solutions. She makes a conscious effort to mould the appearance American self such that it is acceptable to her mainstream American colleagues. She explains that she never wears Indian clothes to her place of work because there are very few Indians in her company. If there had been a few more of them then she would have considered wearing salwar kameez once a week because, 'There is nothing bad in it. They [colleagues] really appreciate it.' Having worked in a small Indian start-up company initially, Mrigakshi was very happy to get a job at a well-known American company like Sabine Information Solutions, but she still keeps to herself. She brings lunch with her every morning, eats on her own at her desk, and seldom ventures into the company cafeteria.

Navneet, a systems analyst in Alliance Core Networks, a computer company in the Silicon Valley, tries hard to fit in with her non-Indian co-workers. She always wears carefully selected Western outfits bought in annual clearance sales in upmarket department stores. There are few Indians in her office and no one in her company wears Indian clothes. She dislikes the idea of 'sticking out like a sore thumb', so she too wears Western clothes to work. However, despite this effort to blend in, she has still not been able to make very many friends at work. She explains, 'There is not much interaction . . . I was totally isolated in the last job'.

In her previous job she was the only person handling the project she had been assigned. She asked to be moved to another group but she is not happy in this new group: 'I am not sure whether there is racial discrimination, but it may turn out to be so'. Most of the people in this group are Israelis. They talk to each other in their own language, ignoring her 'unless there is something specific [to tell her] such as "there is a meeting today",' Navneet complains, 'Day by day it is getting worse'. The Israelis come together, have lunch together, and leave together, leaving Navneet out of everything socially. Navneet finds it 'pretty uncomfortable'.

It is interesting that the only incident of an Indian worker feeling 'pretty uncomfortable' due to social exclusion at the workplace that I have recorded in my interviews was caused by the behaviour of another immigrant group, and this behaviour was not intentional or targeted at my informant specifically. The incidence of racially-motivated action by native-born Americans is minimal in the American workplace, especially in occupations in which at least a graduate degree is required for employment. Moreover, Indian immigrants are especially respected for their technical and scientific skills. My informants sometimes discussed the so-called glass-ceiling, the invisible, yet unbreakable barrier that is said to keep minorities and women from rising to the upper rungs of the corporate ladder, regardless of their qualifications or achievements. However, not a single one of my informants reported having experienced any racial or ethnic discrimination in their place of employment.

My conclusion is that newly arrived immigrants imagine that their familiarity with Western culture has equipped them to deal with life in America, but once they arrive in the US, new immigrants from India are perplexed by their difficulties in socializing with native-born Americans or other ethnic groups resident in the US.

II. MEDIUM DURATION

THE AMERICANIZATION OF THE SELF

Indians who have spent at least two years in the US become familiar with the American accent, linguistic phrases, driving practices, gender interaction expectations, hand gestures, body language, foods, apparel, workplace etiquette, recreational pursuits, holiday traditions, TV shows, sports, and a myriad of other entities that constitute what is commonly referred to as American culture. This makes it easier for them to function in the US. Shupriya says:

After a year or two here, which were spent studying in graduate school, I learnt to function in America. Not just driving, and the accent, etc., I now understand the jokes, and even the references to American TV shows. I can talk to anybody here without any problem.

Rani says:

Coming from India, I was a big cricket fan, but I had no idea about American football or baseball, so it was often difficult to join sports-related conversations, especially at work. So I made a special effort to learn about those sports, and now I keep up with the games and scores, I can easily understand and join in such conversations!

In fact Rani organizes a Super Bowl party at her home every year and is an extremely vocal fan of the local team.

Cultural adjustment occurs in men as well as women. Most of my male informants have learnt the rules of baseball and American football, and they keep abreast of the latest news concerning these games. They keep track of

Hollywood movies and American TV shows. They have learnt to put up tents, start camp-fires, and grill sausages during camping trips. They even take the trash out once a week, and many help with loading the dish-washer daily. Of course, those Indian women who work outside the home are given more opportunities to experience US culture than those who spend most of their time in their homes. In the words of my subjects, Indian working women adjust to the US much faster than Indian non-working women do. Asian Indian immigrant women who are employed outside the home have more money to spend on buying themselves the consumer commodities that signify middle class membership in America.

Lastly, Indian women know that in India, 'decent' women are expected to uphold certain norms, such as maintaining a distance from all men they are not related to, and avoiding alcohol. Recent immigrants still retain these norms. However, immigrant Indian women, especially those who are employed and interact with non-Indians through work, and who have been in the US for a medium duration of time, learn that in America, women are expected to act cordially with men, to make some conversation, and to have at least one alcoholic drink in certain social situations. They learn to avoid being perceived as 'shy' and 'unsociable'.

Desi or NRI: The Contested Self

Adjustment to the US is often accompanied by some amount of emotional withdrawal from 'back home', that is, India. What seemed normal and regular in India no longer seems so, and what seemed strange in America now appears to be acceptable. It sometimes takes an outsider to see what is strange, and having become relative strangers to India, my subjects noticed many discomfiting trends in India. Almost all the women I spoke to constantly made comparisons between their experiences in India and in the US. I had expected to find that most Indian immigrant women were uncomfortable in the US but what I actually found was that the comfort level depended on the duration of residence in the US: the longer the women spent in the US, the more comfortable they became here.

Though this is in many ways wholly predictable, an unexpected finding was that many Indian immigrant women gradually begin to experience a pronounced lack of comfort in India which surfaces during their visits to India. It appears that lack of comfort in India is directly related to the length of residence in the US. Antara, a university professor, says:

In two years, I will have spent as long in California as I spent in India. India seems removed from me the longer I stay here. I've lived in California since 1981. I am not in touch with India anymore. For example: money. A hundred rupees now is nothing, where as it was our monthly stipend when I was there. In that sense, I am getting further and further removed, and what I remember about India is very different from what it is now.

Rani, a research scientist, says, 'We do watch Hindi movies once in a while, but I don't enjoy them. I feel very disconnected from the current Indian movies, so the only Indian movies I enjoy are the older Hindi movies of fifteen to twenty years ago that I can identify with.'

Aparajita, a human resources manager explains that she loves to visit India, but she frequently finds herself chaffing against the absence of good customer service:

Deshe [in India], if you go to the post office, in your whole life you will never see their teeth [never see the postal clerks smile]. If you want an inland letter for ten rupees, they will say, 'Give the exact change'. It is not so much that they want the exact change as it is the brusque manner in which they demand it. On such occasions, one thinks of the post offices here. Here the very first thing they say is, 'Hi! How can I help you?'

Also, on her recent visits to India, Aparajita has found the impractical dress code there quite irritating:

There are no restrictions at home, but of course, I can't roam around in pants in Uluberia [Uluberia is a small town in the rural backwaters of Bengal], though I could do that in Baligunj or New Alipore [these are slightly Westernized, 'modern' middle class and upper middle class neighbourhoods in Kolkata]. Still, I do wear salwar-kameezes, not saris. This time it was awfully hot there.

Though Niharika, a software engineer at Mallory-Powers, is not too concerned about the practical issues Aparajita brings up, she mentions her social unease on her recent visits to India:

The place I worked in Kolkata before I left for the US was a semi-government concern, and people there were pretty old and conservative, and they really hadn't [pause], and this was like five years back, so women software engineers were fewer than now. So they were not really used to working with girls. So I think that made all the difference.... [I was] more of an exhibit, and people don't really believe that you are an engineer. And there, it's like a different world.

She explains that in Kolkata she believed that every woman should be the centre of her home and family, but now she knows that a woman can be much more than this. She feels that she was being trained to live her life in certain manner, but now knows that it is not the only way to live her life:

For generations people have been feeding you things about women being the centre of the family, of the home. Those things I think tend to matter less in this country [the US]. I mean, you know that they are important, but they are not important in the same way as was portrayed to you back in Kolkata.

Mrigakshi, the software tester at Sabine Information Solutions, and her husband want to return to India permanently within a few years. Mrigakshi however is concerned that now she has become used to the comfort and independence of living in the US, she will find it difficult to readjust to life in India:

We plan to go back to India for good after about five years. But after five years, when I really have to go back, I don't know how much I will be accepting the thing. It's now in the mind that I will return, but how many compromises I will have to make at the actual time of return!

Mrigakshi believes that in some ways, she is happier here in the US than in India for in the US she can escape the interference of family members, and avoid 'the nuisance that relatives occasionally make of themselves'. She says:

I definitely think that after staying here for a few years I have developed a bad habit, I feel irritated if relatives interfere too much in my affairs. That is a very big point because it causes a lot of problems for a lot of people. Once you get into the habit of living on your own [pause], here no one [else] gets to know anything at all.

Shupriya, a systems auditor in the Bay Area, misses her parents and siblings in Delhi very much. When she lost her husband three years ago, she thought of moving back to Delhi, but ultimately she stayed on in the US because she came to the conclusion that there are things which would not be available to her in India. For example, she takes her personal freedom and ability to make career choices for granted in the US, but this would become limited in India's conservative society.

Amitava Kumar writes of how immigrants from the Indian subcontinent are released from the grip of rigid traditions and fixed cultural habits when they settle in the new country, so they are able to construct a new self. Kumar stresses the freedom to be oneself in the diaspora, 'In the diaspora, especially, culture and lives can, and often do, find new undiscovered forms. So that immigrants balance the conceit of a preserved heritage against the unanticipated and fairly uncanny elaboration of new identities that are liberating' (2000: 229).

Navneet is a computer systems programmer at Alliance Core Networks. She is in her late twenties and has been married to Gurdeep for a little more than two years. She loves to visit India, and in fact would be happy to return to India permanently. However, her visits to India are not entirely enjoyable, for she cannot spend her entire vacation with her mother and her grandparents at Chandigarh, Punjab. As the *bahu* (daughter-in-law) of her husband's family, she is expected to spend a considerable chunk of her time in India at her *sasural* (the home of her parents-in-law) in Patiala, a small town in

Punjab. Navneet's mother is a professor in Punjab University, and so she is a very liberal and understanding woman. Navneet says, 'I talk very freely with my parents'. But Navneet's mother-in-law on the other hand, is 'conservative'. She expects Navneet to say *Hanji, hanji* (Yes, Yes) to her all the time, she wants Navneet to behave in a meek and deferential manner towards all of her elders in her *sasural*. Navneet therefore feels her that husband's family is different from her own family although fortunately, Gurdeep is not as conservative as they are. Though Navneet's mother has visited them in the US, Gurdeep's parents have never done so; Navneet says they are too old to travel. In the US, Navneet does not have to worry about Gurdeep's family's expectations, but it is a different story during her visits to India. She avoids spending too much time at the *sasural*—she spent two days there after her wedding, and ten days during a recent visit to India—but she is made to feel guilty for not spending longer there. It is this difficult part of her vacation which prevents her from being entirely comfortable in India.

Shreya is a research scientist in a biopharmaceutical company in the Bay Area. She is in her mid-twenties. She is married, and has been resident in the US for three years. She mentions that she missed India very much when she first set up home in this country, but her very first vacation in India helped her realize that there are many advantages of living in the US. For example, upon returning to India for her annual vacation, she was struck by how relatively limited and dangerous the road-system is in India—she fondly remembered the frequent road-trips she and her husband are in the habit of taking in the US, driving to popular area attractions and awesome natural parks within a couple of hours from her home in the San Francisco Bay Area. Now she appreciates the benefits of living in the US:

I didn't realize that, like, living here [US] [pause], until I returned *deshe* [homeland] for the first time, I used to always tell Gautam [her husband] that we will stay here only for a few years. As soon as we have saved some money, we will return to India. When I went back to India I realized that here we take a lot of things for granted that we will not get in India.

All the women I have quoted here currently experience levels of discomfort that they had not previously felt in India. Before, it was their home and so most things there seemed natural and proper, and even if everything did not feel completely right, the women did not notice it, or think too much about it. Now that they have been exposed to the new culture of the US, they notice things that seem wrong or out of place in India. This is because their sensibilities have changed though the change has been profound in some cases and subtle in others. While many of the women I interviewed say that America is their home now, others feel that that they belong to both India and America; they have no single or true home anymore. A third group consists of women who still consider India their home, but none of them accept India unquestioningly in the way that they did before. In fact, while it is true that Indian immigrants use Indian standards to understand America, it is also true that while in *desh* (India), they use standards acquired in America to judge India. I believe that immigrant experience not only in America, but also in India, is the site for self-contention, for a contest between Indian and American sensibilities. The experiences and emotions of Indian immigrants in both countries are also the location of the process of the construction of the immigrant self: a self that is neither Indian nor American but caught between the two.

Adjustment to the US lifestyle is achieved by subtle as well as radical changes in social behaviour, role playing, and presentation of self. As Goffman (1959) has argued, all social contact, whether public or private, is a dramaturgical production in which the self is presented. Cooley (1902) and Mead (1934) have also emphasized the importance of role playing and social exchange communicated through symbolic interaction. The subjects of my research learned to modify the presentation of their selves in light of the fact that their audience was no longer Indian but American. Dramaturgical changes in the histrionic production of self were accompanied by learning the symbolic meanings of words and actions unique to the US. Within a few years of arrival in the US, my interviewees became quite familiar with the shared symbolic systems of American culture. Naturally, the degree to which they succeeded in mastering American culture depended on many variables, such as previous knowledge of Western culture, type of occupation, time spent in the American workplace, and so on; new American roles were adopted, and former Indian ones were often abandoned. New local role models emerged. Of course, familiarity is not enough for competence is also required. Most respondents reported that it took a few years to attain competence in the new roles. The internal psyche remained Indian, but the external 'Me' becomes significantly American in this early stage of residence in the US.

RECONCILING THE AMERICAN AND THE INDIAN SELF

This study revealed that after a few years in the US, having experienced living and functioning in America, the interviewees found it easier to enjoy the freedom of individual choice, unbridled consumerism, and economic ease of living that had attracted them to US in the first place. For example, having spent two years in the US, Kanchana says:

I have just commenced an M.B.A. in the University of California at Irvine. I have taken an apartment there, I will share it with another girl. I will drive to the Bay Area in weekends, so that I can spend the weekends with my husband. My husband is paying for everything. Can you imagine such an arrangement in India? His family would have squelched the whole thing at once, and so would mine!

Despite substantial Americanization during the medium duration stage of the development of immigrant consciousness, a large percentage of day-to-day behaviour and thought continues to be Indian. We observe from Mrigakshi's example, despite her attraction to American cultural objects and consumer items, she retained considerable Indianness in her food, clothes, recreational choices, and so on. For example, she and her husband continue to cook and eat a lot of Indian food, she wears Indian clothes at home, especially at the weekends when she and her husband frequently get-together with their friends, all of whom are Indians. Mrigakshi does puja every day, and she fasts on Fridays for Santoshi Ma. So her spiritual self continues to be Hindu.

Another common issue I came across was difficulty in code-switching and role-changing, that is, changing from the role of an Indian American working woman to that of an immigrant wife and mother, and using the obligatory cultural codes of each of these roles in the requisite social context. Ankita says:

The most difficult moment is when I come back from work to face my children, and my parents-in-law. My husband comes home from work much later. I feel like I have to shed not only my business suit and wear a salwar kameez, or an Indian tailored all-concealing housecoat, but I also have to shed my American attitude, the assertiveness that I pride myself upon in my office.

One might therefore ask how Mrigakshi reconciles her new found American tastes, behavioural habits, and nascent American identity, with the remnants of her Indian identity? It seems that Mrigakshi has considerable difficulty in switching between her Indian and her American identity as was evident from her unease concerning junctures and meeting points, and the suture joining her Indian and American selves. For example, she spoke to me at length about her husband's office Christmas party. She said she felt strange in her colourful silk sari and heavy gold jewellery, especially since she was surrounded by American women wearing mostly short Black dresses, and subtle diamond jewellery, 'But I still think I should wear a sari, after all it is a formal party. Actually I don't think even a salwar kameez would be decent.'

Whether formal or informal, westernized outfits are the dress code for the role of the Indian American working woman. On the other hand, salwar kameezes, saris, and cover-all housecoats stitched in India are the dress code for the role of the Indian immigrant wife and mother. My informants seems to be set upon following these codes as best as they could, and they did their best to switch between them whenever required.

The drive to fulfil behavioural expectations while in the American public gaze and to be accepted at the workplace is a powerful incentive for mimicking American standards of dress and deportment. Yet, in private moments, and within diasporic gatherings, medium duration Asian Indians relax into old habits of clothing, speech, recreation, and consumption. The pattern seems to be the same for both men and women, but it is more prevalent in female immigrants. Indian women are the standard bearers of culture: they wear saris and salwar kameez, cook Indian dishes, decorate the home with Indian artefacts, and acculturate the children in Indian languages, religion, and culture; hence it is they who bear the responsibility to deploy ethnic culture. It follows that in the diaspora too, women perform Indian culture more than men do. Wherever she is situated, the *Bharatiya nari* (Indian woman) is always held responsible for upholding *Bharatiya parampara* (Indian culture).

III. LONG DURATION

Americanization versus Indianization

As time passes in the new country Indian immigrant women, especially working Indian immigrant women, become more and more American. As their familiarity with American culture increases due to day-to-day interaction with it, they internalize it. A significant portion of their Indianness and its accompanying ideology and behaviours fades away as their participation in Indian culture decreases.

However, as previously discussed, Indian immigrant women do not lose touch with their Indian self completely, for their sensibilities have been shaped in India, by Indian values and mores. Despite many immigrant decades out of India, and many overlying layers of American socialization, this cannot be undone. The presence of fellow immigrants from India, as well as the increasing awareness that mainstream Americans will always see the Indian diaspora as immigrants, means that the Indian self persists. Sometimes being seen primarily as an Indian is caused by positive essentialization, but even if such a gaze is motivated by friendly interest in India and Indians, essentialization nevertheless causes psychic dissonance. In fact, essentialization (sometimes positive, but more often pejorative) is a common experience of minority immigrants in the West (Espiritu 2003). In the face of this, Indians embrace their Indian self and consciously represent their native culture, whilst simultaneously educating their children in it (Roy 1988) with the result that recursive patterns of Indianness emerge.

The transmission of Indian culture is usually through its regional or parochial manifestations. Most Indian immigrants in the US are more involved in the activities of their regional culture organizations, such as the American Telugu Association, the North American Bengali Association, or the Maharashtra Mandal Committee, than in pan-Indian organizations such as the Federation of Indians in America, or the Alliance of Indians in America. The closest circle of friends of most first generation Indian immigrants invariably consists of other Indians who hails from the same region of India from which they themselves originate. This helps to embrace not just the Indian self, but more specifically, the parochial self, and the immigrant children are also trained in the parochial culture of their parents' state or region of origin in India. Hence, in the San Francisco Bay Area, immigrant Telugu children attend weekly Telugu language classes, immigrant Bengali children learn Rabindra Sangeet, and immigrant Marathi children learn to dance the Lavani.

As discussed by Mrigakshi, Shreya, Niharika, Rani, and Navneet earlier in this chapter, lack of comfort with the roles the Indian immigrant is expected to play and with American culture are a hallmark of the first stage of self development. We can compare this with attitudes in the third stage. In this last phase, immigrants are very familiar with American culture, having had a lengthy residence and tenure of employment in the US.

Megha explains herself in the following way:

I had been in college [in the US] . . . I think I learnt how to deal with people's ignorance of India, of the 'Third World'. I learnt how to cope much better by the time I was in graduate school. I learnt pretty well. . . . It depends, sometimes I ignore, sometimes I explain, sometimes I get irritated, you know. But usually, and this I am sure is because I came here so early, I usually don't feel like a foreigner.

Megha is not perturbed in the least by this juggling of roles and identities, in fact she revels in it. Sometimes the switch of identities is conscious, but at most times it is not, 'So I do both [present herself both as an insider and an outsider to her American colleagues and students]. And I'm not entirely sure that it's very conscious, sometimes it is conscious, but I don't think it usually is.' In spite of the constant shuffling between identities, or maybe because of it, Megha feels that as far as her identity is concerned, she has come into her own in the last few years: 'Now I'm thirty-seven, I feel that in the last few years I have come into an identity, which I think is a truly, the trendy word I guess is transnational.'

Megha believes that rather than being a drawback, her lack of commitment to any single identity or cultural framework is her principle strength. She identifies her ability to survive anywhere, in any culture, and to regain her well-being however many times she is uprooted and replanted, as her chief virtue.

Like Megha, Urmila too has been in the US since undergraduate college where she was a premedical student at Brandeis University before she went to Medical School at Imperial College, London. Internal medicine is her field of specialization. She and her husband moved to California after a short spell in the UK because they wanted to settle there. Having worked at King's Medical Group for many years, Urmila now runs two practices of her own, both of which are shared with one other physician. Urmila does not display exactly the same self in her clinic and at home for she, for example, wears shirts and trousers to the clinic, but wears saris or salwar kameezes in most Indian get-togethers. However, rather than pointing out the different selves she presents to different audiences, Urmila prefers to emphasize the continuities in her selfhood:

I don't try to develop an American accent like I know some people consciously do, or unconsciously. I just basically . . . I'm Indian, I'm a doctor. And I think Indian doctors are kind of respected by Americans almost because they usually tend to be very good. And it hasn't really been an issue. All this stuff is atypical a little because if I was in a big computer firm, having to talk to clients, I might project myself differently.

Urmila believes that she has a single cohesive identity, that of an Indian immigrant doctor, and so everything she does, even in her roles of wife, mother, sister, daughter, and friend, is subsumed in that one main identity. When I asked her to describe herself she said:

Immigrant, doctor . . . and I am quite comfortable being that. Okay. And I always stipulate that this is California and the Bay Area. And if I had ended up in Idaho or some place like that, [in the] middle of Iowa, middle of farmland, then it would be totally different.

Urmila is explaining that because she is based in the Bay Area, in California, her work life allows her a certain amount of freedom. Due to the diasporic nature of the region, the Bay Area allows her the freedom to be an immigrant, hence she does not have to try to be American. Her accent may be different, her name may be difficult for non-Indians to pronounce, but her patients and her fellow physicians are accepting of this because a lot of immigrants in California bear similar characteristics. Their non-Americanisms are tolerated because they are very skilled in their respective professions. The same holds true for Indians in the tech industry and in scientific research and development.

Of course, Urmila's many decades in the US have worn away much of her Indian ideology and behaviour and so the tensions between the two selves are lessened. In Urmila's words:

Neither of us [Urmila and her husband] is very religious. We do go to the Puja [Durga Puja, a Bengali religious festival], but not every time. Depending on what else we are doing over the weekend. All that. But that's not so important to us.

About her children, Urmila says:

I think my children are missing out a bit on Indian culture, Indian history, but you know, they learn a lot of it because we have Indian friends who keep going back and forth. We go back and forth. I think you can't expect the children to know as much about Indian life as kids there. But since they are going to be just basically Americans, I think it's fine, whatever amount they know.

These are pragmatic words from a woman who is speaking from the perspective of being in the midst of raising children in the US. The contrast between Urmila's self-assured belief in the correctness of making sure her children are well adjusted in the US rather than Indianized, with the overanxious imaginings of Niharika, the software engineer at Mallory Powers who has been in the US only three years and has not yet had any children is very marked: 'I feel that if you are here, the children suffer a lot. They are kind of neither here nor there.' The research of Bandana Purkayastha on the children of foreign-born South Asian immigrant parents is relevant to the issue of raising children of Asian Indian descent in the US. Purkayastha has shown that second-generation South Asian Americans traverse a transnational world by constructing multilayered ethnic identities that are fluid and fragmented. Children of immigrants negotiate the socio-political and cultural constraints they encounter in their daily-lives by activating various co-existing layers of their highly nuanced ethnic identities in different cultural contexts (2005).

However, in spite of Urmila's confidence in the balance of Indian and American influences on her children, and despite her projection of an integrated personality, there is a major contradiction in her life. On the one hand, she says that Indians have not assimilated enough, and they stick to friends within their own ethnic community. On the other hand, Urmila acknowledges that her children do not get as much Indian culture as she would perhaps like, in spite of having Indian friends and frequent visits to India. Perhaps it is between these contradictions that Urmila and her family have found a balanced niche for themselves.

Shupriya came to the US at the age of 23. She has now spent eighteen years in the US as a systems auditor. Shupriya seems to have gained a certain amount of skill in juggling her American self with her Indian self. She appears to have gotten used to being the natural representative of India by virtue of being the only Indian in the room.

Shupriya feels that there is a certain amount of conscious role playing in her persona. She is conscious of playing the role of the 'Indian woman' in her interaction with Americans, but of course, this interaction is possible only because she has learnt enough of American culture to be comfortable with mainstream Americans. Having grown up in India, she knows far more about India that all her non-Indian friends and acquaintances and so she is not surprised that she has been ascribed this role: 'I'm definitely Indian. I've lived here for half my life, I came here when I was twenty-three, but I have twenty-three years of [Indian] culture ingrained into me'. However, due to her Westernized upbringing, and almost 20 years living in the US, she is very comfortable in the US:

I am equally at home with pretty much anyone. I don't have a problem dressing up in a sari because I don't think I look good in a strapless evening gown. I think when I was slimmer I could have gotten away with it. Yeah, I felt bad, just as I would have felt bad if there was female infanticide here. Yeah, as an Indian, yeah, you feel a little bad, but it doesn't bother me.

Prototypes

I noted in the course of my interviews that many, if not most of my informants used prototypes of what Americans and Indian immigrants were like, and they used these prototypes to distinguish so-called 'typical' American behavioural norms from Indian immigrant ones. In fact, a few adjectives such as 'honest', 'cordial', 'punctual', 'fun-loving', and 'self-oriented' always came up when Americans were being discussed by my interviewees. In contrast, adjectives such as 'hard-working', 'respectful', 'frugal', 'unpunctual', and 'family-oriented' often came up when my interviewees talked about members of their own community.

Though most of my interviewees built up prototypes of Indian and American, they would proceed to tell me how they were different from the prototypical Indian immigrant. This happened with almost all the women I interviewed and observed. Shupriya was perhaps the most articulate on this issue: 'This is my theory: I think Indians as individuals are very confident of themselves, but as a group, I don't think that they have a group identity . . . Americans as a group are very proud of their country . . . I think Indians as a whole lack that.' Shupriya also said that she found that Indians in America tended to characterize different communities in their stereotypical form: 'Sometimes I find that Indians are also very colour conscious: "Blacks are like this, Chinese are like that".' Shupriya has a prototype of what 'typical' Indian Americans are like: ashamed of India and also racially chauvinistic. She is of course careful to point out that she herself is different. The observations of Jean Bacon, another ethnographer of Asian Indian immigrants in the US, reiterate my findings:

Although family members clearly understand and use prototypes of 'Indian' and 'Americans', their use of these prototypes is lucid and creative; they are not overly concerned with living out the symbolic prototypes that form the community's shared understanding of what it means to be an Indian immigrant in America. (1996: 245)

Racialization of Indian Immigrants in America: the Brown Body

The issue of race and the Indian immigrant self tends to be marked by ideas about who *we* are *not*, rather than who *they* actually *are*. Luhrmann has said:

Identity politics are politics of difference, in which the central desperate question is how to negotiate confident uniqueness in a hostile world that threatens to obliterate you. Indeed if you search for identity in the classic psychoanalysis texts such as Fenichel's you will find no listing for it in the index. (1996: 199)

Vijay Prashad helps us to understand how Indians in the US are anxious to avoid being seen as Black, for the Blacks are perceived to be at the bottom of the race hierarchy in the US. In fact, the whole purpose of the emphasis on ethnic identity is to demarcate difference from Blacks:

Desis seek out an authentic culture for complex reasons, among them the desire not to be seen as fundamentally inferior to those who see themselves as 'white' and superior. To be on par with or at least not beneath these people, desis, like other subordinated peoples, revel in those among them who succeed in white terms. There is a *sotto voce* knowledge among non-whites of their various forms of greatness. (2000: 157)

There are serious reasons to doubt the 'clash of civilizations' theory first proposed by Samuel Huntington (1996), and subsequently elaborated by others who espouse the singularity of identity and the inevitability of conflict based on that identity. Humans are complex beings composed of many identities and so we must recognize the plurality of such. Identity is affected by many factors such as citizenship, residence, geographic origin, gender, class, occupation, religious beliefs, and even leisure time activities. It is our responsibility to ascertain what our relevant identities are, and to make use of reasoning and choice to weigh the relative importance of these different identities. I found that my subjects usually attempted to resist imposed identities. They wanted to move beyond external attempts to incarcerate and miniaturize their selves by narrow divisions of ethno-racial characteristics, nation states, religious affiliations, or even civilizations.

After a decade or more in the US, Indian professional working women become more adept at maintaining an American identity. They are at ease in America, they adopt American food and dress habits, and American media is usually their entertainment of choice. They keep track of American sports, political events, and those who have been naturalized exercise their franchise. Most Indian professionals resident for a long time are single or joint owners of some real estate and movable property in the US. While familiarity with

America and Americanness increases with length of residence and employment, Indians in America also come to realize that on account of being an ethnic minority, they occupy a subordinate place in the American race/class hierarchy. Espiritu calls this the principle of differential inclusion, 'a process whereby a group of people is deemed integral to the nation, but integral only or precisely because of their designated subordinate standing' (2003: 211). The awareness that minority immigrants in America cannot escape racialization is a constant challenge to the Indian immigrant's sense of self. Despite self-denial of racination, the American subalternity of Brown people cannot be ignored.

My respondents reported that in their experience, the social exclusion of Brown people ranges from subtle to crude. In fact, I am not certain that the instances of social exclusion that my informants related were actually due to racial or ethnic prejudice, but these incidents are worth discussing all the same, for they are typical of the social hurdles faced by first generation Indian immigrants in the US.

Navneet spoke of how she was excluded from the sought after, usually White, social cliques in college. She was convinced that her exclusion was on account of her race and ethnicity. However, this argument can be refuted since she did not have any proof that it was her racial character that caused her to be shut out of the popular circles of friendship in the American college where she obtained her Master's degree in computer sciences.

In another possible instance of social exclusion due to racial and ethnic chauvinism, Rani mentioned how she was left out of social get-togethers at work. Often her White colleagues would congregate in a bar, or at a sport event outside work hours, and Rani was seldom invited. Also, she herself opted out of many work-related parties because she had to return home to her family, and she also often had prior social commitments with Indian family friends. She found that unlike first generation minority immigrants like herself, second generation Indian Americans born and raised in America found it easier to penetrate social cliques. It can be argued that Rani herself opted out of most social events at work due to family commitments, and hence, it was her choice to exclude herself from the joint social activities of her colleagues, but I am not sure.

Rupa spoke of how a homeless White man travelling with her by BART (Bay Area Rapid Transport) shouted, 'Go back to the country you came from!' and threw some half-eaten food at her face. Niharika related an incident about an elderly White colleague at work who, when she told him that her brother had obtained a graduate scholarship to a prestigious American university, said something about 'Students from other countries are taking over the American universities'. She said: 'I suppose he had children of his own who were having a hard time getting into good universities or getting scholarships, but why be rude about my brother?'

Professionally qualified Indians are usually from upper or middle class families in India. Born in the post-colonial era, they are unused to dealing with 'foreigners', White or other, yet growing up in a nation with a perpetual colonial hangover, their sensibilities have been 'Westernized'.

Under first the East Indian Company and then the British Raj, the Indian bourgeoisie 'Brown sahibs' helped to perpetuate colonial rule by acting as intermediaries between the Indian masses and their White masters. As a consequence of their admiration for the British Raj, they began to identify with their colonial masters, and became quite Western in their moral values and day-to-day habits. Though the women and children in this class continued to favour native Indian language, dress, and food, the men were effectively deracinized, and they usually dressed in Western clothes, ate Western food, and spoke, read, and wrote fluent English. Most significantly, their thought processes became quite Westernized.

Most professionally qualified and highly educated middle class modern-day Indians are the descendants of this class of native Indian colonial bourgeoisie. Indian immigrants to the US are also drawn from the progeny of colonial bourgeoisie. In India, their family connections, their English fluency, their multiple educational qualifications, and their professional occupations assured them an elite status; they were unquestionably *bhadrolok* (gentlemen). However, gentility does not ensure adequate employment. The high rate of unemployment and underemployment pushed the educated elite out of India, and their Westernized sensibilities and familiarity with the English language drew them to England and America. Once in the US, Indian immigrants are racialized to 'brownness'. Individuals who would have described themselves in India as 'fair', 'wheat complexioned', or 'golden complexioned' (phrases that are commonly used in English language matrimonial advertisements in Indian newspapers), are forced to describe themselves as 'Brown' or a 'racial minority' in the US for they stand out on account of their dark skin colour. The new global economy is also as racialized as earlier economic formations. As Howard Winant has shown, both the North-South and East-West lines of division are drawn in accordance with racial differences in that, 'The international division of labour, the flow of commodities and capital in trade, and the global movement of people are organized racially' (2004: xx). Asian Indians always suffer on account of their skin colour. Before immigration, Indians did not feel targeted by racism since there were many persons poorer and darker than themselves in India. In the US, the seat of capitalist power, they have a closer view of racism, for there are few whom they have the power to exclude.

Ananya Bhattacharya has written that while the bourgeoisie of the developing world was in a dominant position in its native land, upon migration to the US, it is forced into subordination to the local bourgeoisie. Preferring 'ex-nomination', that is to remain without a name, the developing world bourgeoisie sees itself as universal (1992: 19–46). It seems however that universality is the domain only of Whites, hence Indians in America must resign themselves to being seen not by universal standards, but primarily as Browns. This is especially galling as almost all Indians came to the US of their own volition in an attempt to improve their economic situation.

Being seen as a Brown by the general populace leads to a process of self-recognition on the part of Indians in the US. Identity seems to become centred on a hitherto insignificant quality: the chromatic grade of one's skin. It is true that there are various shades of Brown or 'persons of colour', but it is doubtful that any Indian would identify himself as a Brown. Rather, he would describe himself on the basis of their caste, religion, education, income, occupation, or place of residence (George 1997).

I asked all of my interviewees, 'How do you see yourself in the larger scheme of things? If someone were to ask you out of the blue, "Who are you?", then what would you answer?' Though unused to thinking about such existential questions, most of my interviewees thought about it for a while, and most of the long duration immigrants came up with an answer that approximated to what can be considered to be a statement of Indianness in the US. Indianness is chosen as the principal self-marker mainly because it rejects a subordinate racial position in the US. Indians in America avoid racialization but if race is to be discussed, then Indianness can be linked to an 'Aryan heritage', which is deemed to be preferable to 'brownness', or being a racial minority. George questions Indian links to an 'Aryan' heritage, but she notes that Indian Americans favour an imputed genetic and cultural connection to Aryanness. She argues, 'What is refused by nearly all upper and middle class South Asians is not so much a specific racial identity, as the idea of being raced. The only identity that is acknowledged is the cultural and ethnic one of being no more and no less than "Indian-American"', and 'when pressed, the commonly offered affiliation approaching a racial category that is seen as acceptable is "Aryan"' (1997: 31).

George identifies two main reasons why first generation Indian immigrants are reluctant to racialize themselves: (a) In post-colonial India, 'caste, class, religion, and region together provide ample markers of identity that result in intricate social hierarchies' (hence, race is an inadequate marker of Indian immigrant identity, for religion, caste, education, employment of parents, family connections, region of origin, and native language are equally important), and (b) in the present Californian political environment, where there is a concerted effort to reduce the privileges of illegal as well as legal Brown people, there is even more reason to sidestep 'issues concerning both skin colour and race'. Thus today's 'colourblind' politics of California, as evident in Proposition 209 (also known as the California Civil Rights Initiative), is especially appealing to Indian immigrants, for it helps them to 'avoid self-identification by skin-colour or race' (1997: 31–2). Proposition

209 is a California ballot proposition which was approved in November 1996. It was opposed by proponents of affirmative action because it amended the state constitution to prohibit state government institution from looking at race, sex, or ethnicity, in the spheres of public employment, public contracting or public education. In general, African Americans in California had gained far more from affirmative action programmes than Asian Americans. Affirmative action programmes lost the support of the people of California in the mid-1990s, and such programmes were discontinued by the state government. Hence race became irrelevant in university admissions, government employment, and award of government contracts to small businesses. This suited Indian immigrants very well, for they wanted to be recognized for their achievements, and rise above any loss of status associated with their race or ethnicity.

Relevant to this discussion of race relations, I found that whilst a few of my informants did mention incidents in which they had been targeted by race and ethnicity related social exclusion in the US, none of them reported experiencing any racial or ethnic discrimination in their place of work. Though seemingly reluctant to discuss any bigotry they themselves might have been the victim of, some of my interviewees described instances of racial prejudice that *other* Indian immigrants in their acquaintance had suffered. While Asian Indians do boast the highest median household income for any ethnic group in the country, this piece of data ignores the possibility that their incomes may be lower than whites with similar educations and degrees. On the whole, my discussants narrated fewer stories of racial or ethnic narrow-mindedness than I had predicted. This trend can be related to my hypothesis that not only are Indian immigrants treated cordially by most Americans, but also, Indian immigrants who have come to the US of their own volition, and who have stayed on here of their own choosing find it difficult for them to admit that they do indeed experience racial slights in the US.

Stuart Hall writes of how Blacks in Britain learned to embrace this imposed term as a mark of self-identification, and how they gradually came to unite under the banner of 'Black people' in order to fight for racial equality, 'Black was created as a political category', it entailed a 'change of self-recognition, a new process of identification and the emergence of visibility of a new subject, a subject that was always there, but emerging historically' (1991: 54).

Hall's description and analysis of the emergence of diasporic Black identity in Britain is instructive. However, it must be noted that unlike Blacks in Britain, Indian immigrants in the US have seldom embraced, or even accepted, the idea of a Brown identity. Rather, I have detected a tendency to sidestep Brown racialization, and instead opt for an emphasis on diasporic or Asian Indian ethnic identity. Hence this study will now move to discuss racial strategies adopted by Indian immigrants in the US that are deployed in order to circumvent such categorization.

Racial Strategies of Indian Americans

In the pre-civil rights era, Asian Indians aimed at being racially designated as 'White'. For a brief period between 1908 and 1922, the American courts even granted naturalization and US citizenship to Asian Indians on the basis of this designation. At that time, only those held to be White were eligible for naturalization but between 1908 and 1922, there were 69 Asian Indians who successfully petitioned the courts. They argued that since Indians were of Aryan stock, they should be classified as Caucasians and since Caucasian was synonymous with White, they were eligible for naturalization. The American judiciary approved their petition, declaring that the term 'White' was used to distinguish Caucasians from the Mongolian and Negro races. As Indians belonged to neither of these categories, they should be considered 'White', and hence they should be allowed to undergo the process of naturalization (Jensen 1988). In fact, Asian Indians and their descendants were categorized as 'White' right up to 1974 and it was only in the mid-1970s that the racial strategy of immigrant Indians underwent a radical change. Post civil rights movement legislation motivated Indian Americans to lobby for minority status and the affirmative action programmes that went with it. They campaigned strenuously, and the Census authority moved Asian Indians from the 'White' category to the Asian/Pacific Islander category in 1974. By 1982 Asian Indians qualified for American programmes meant for minorities who had been historically discriminated against.

Thus the racial strategy of the Indian immigrant community underwent a convenient shift from passing themselves off as Whites to identifying themselves as Asians. They have not received many benefits however because Asian Americans form a group that is too diffuse and too loosely connected to wield much influence. Most Asian American communities, that is Chinese, Indians, Koreans, Filipinos, Japanese, and Vietnamese people in America, do have a few things in common. For example, they usually align themselves with the predominantly White majority establishment that occupies most positions of power in the US. They rarely make common cause with Blacks and Hispanics, thus most Asian immigrant groups, including Indian Americans, supported Proposition 209 (California Civil Rights Act) that ended affirmative action in university admission policies. This study shows that, like many other Asian ethnics in America, Indian immigrants in the US prefer to associate with Whites and co-ethnics. Indian Americans are often chauvinists themselves, and they have been found to dislike social interaction with Blacks and Hispanics to the point that many of my interviewees expressed relief at the comparatively small number of Blacks in California.

Equally, Meera Nair's movie *Mississippi Masala* portrays the Indian community's shameful fear of racial miscegenation with Blacks. Almost 38 per cent of the population of California consists of people of Hispanic or Latino origin. I observed in my own research that interaction with, or imitation of, Hispanics is seldom welcomed by first generation Indian immigrants. Ankita says, 'I don't want to send my kids to the local high school, Hermosa High School, because there are too many Hispanics there!' Zarika, a second generation Indian American girl notes that Indian parents in the US are determined to get their offspring married to suitable Indian Hindu matches, and they are vehemently opposed to any friendship with Blacks or Hispanics, 'Hindu Indians who speak the same language and are of the same caste are considered the perfect match, Whites are good, Asians are okay, but a Black or Latino girlfriend or boyfriend is considered a grave disappointment, and of course Muslims are a big no-no!'

As we can see from the above anecdote, the Indian immigrant community is quite insular, but it makes an exception in the case of Whites and other Asian Americans, and approves of friendships with them. Furthermore, academic logistics often force Asian American scholars of different ethnicities to congregate in the same department in American universities. UC Berkeley's Centre of South and South-East Asian Studies, and San Francisco State University's Department of Asian Studies are examples from the Bay Area. This may sometimes foster alliances between US resident scholars of various Asian ethnicities. Lastly, Asian Americans of different nationalities have sometimes united to oppose discrimination, prejudice, and racist crimes against Asian Americans.

Espiritu explains that as they are 'Administratively treated as a homogeneous group, Asian Americans found it necessary to respond as a group' (1992: 163). The US Census Bureau proposed to group all Asians into a single category for the Census of 1980 and 1990 and there was going to be no breakdown of that category into its constituent nations of origin. However, due to synchronized efforts by Asian American community leaders originating from different (Asian) nations, the US Census Bureau agreed to include a detailed enumeration of each Asian subgroup in the Census.

As Espiritu points out, on the whole, Indian immigrants have been eager to join in the Asian American pan-ethnic effort to fight for the individual and united interests of the various groups of Asian Americans in the US. In the 1980s, 'Dotbusters' indulged in random violence against Indian immigrants in the US (the 'dot' refers to the bindi, decorative mark worn in the middle of the forehead by Indian women, especially Hindus). On 27 September 1987, Navroze Mody, a 31-year old man of Indian (Parsee) origin, was badly mauled by a gang of White and Hispanic youths. He died a few days later in the hospital. This incident took place in Hoboken, New Jersey (Misir 1996). The urge to protect the Indian community from such racially motivated violence prompted Indian immigrant leaders to join the pan-ethnic Asian American struggle to halt anti-Asian violence in the US.

Diasporic/Transnational Self

It is difficult to sustain pan-Asian American alliances so Indian Americans make efforts to build up a diasporic, *pravasi* (the Hindi word for diasporic), or ethnic, Indian identity. The word diaspora refers to the dispersion or spread of any people from their original homeland. Such people naturally experience divided loyalties, for they have emotional ties both to their country of origin as well as to their host country. Sometimes they form associations that lobby in the new country for objectives in the old homeland. Thus, a triadic relationship is formed between the diaspora, the nation of their current residence, and their original home country. Based in homes both 'here' and 'there', diasporic people are forced to maintain multiple identities that link them variously with different nationalities, races, and ethnicities. Multiple identities and numerous homelands are useful for navigating the contrary global political and economic situations that mark the life of a transnational. Globalization of culture helps to maintain a multifocal identity, just as objects, images, and meanings move back and forth between various nations. Transnational people are also trans-cultural. Not only are they fluent in more than one language, diasporic people are also fluent in more than one culture, and they have the ability to syncretically fuse heterogeneous cultural parts into a wholly new configuration.

In the first issue of *Diaspora: A Journal of Transnational Studies*, William Safran defined diaspora as people who have themselves been, or whose ancestors have been, 'dispersed from a specific original "centre" to two or more "peripheral", or foreign regions'. Safran emphasized that such people 'retain a collective memory' of the homeland, they want to eventually return to it 'when conditions are appropriate', and they continue to relate, 'personally or vicariously' to the centre of origin (1991: 83–9).

The Indian immigrants I interviewed did not like to see themselves as Brown (Americans) or racial minorities, instead they consider themselves diasporic Indians. Racialization to 'brownness' locates them at a comparative disadvantage in class formations in the US. In comparison to the negative experiences of exclusion and discrimination that a racialized minority status brings, diasporic consciousness serves to provide a positive identity. Building upon strengths such as the rich cultural heritage of India and its current popularity in the international milieu, the majority of Indian immigrants in the US have a dual vision of themselves: as immigrants who own houses in the US, but who are not 'at home' here. They are Non-Resident Indians (NRIs) whose hearts reside in their 'true home', which is India. The self of such individuals is constituted of multifocal incongruencies that are blended to form a syncretic whole. Marked by what Paul Gilroy calls 'double consciousness', that is, consciousness both as Americans and as ethnic Indians, Indian immigrants are very much aware of the contradictions between their residential and diasporic loyalties (1993). Yet, they are hopeful that their membership of both their nation of residence on the one hand, and their country of origin on the other, will help them to manoeuvre themselves to positions of power and influence in both societies.

Ulf Hannerz writes of the experience of the diaspora, 'In a way, all other things being equal, we may increasingly be who we are and want to be, wherever we are' (2002: 227). Due to advances in technology, we have seen that mass media, and also small-scale personal media allow relationships to exist regardless of the separation of thousands of miles. Frequent travel, cable/satellite television, and DVD/video rentals, etc., may make a location that is halfway across the world seem more familiar than the neighbour's home (2002).

Globalization has made it easy to maintain a diasporic identity. While in America, Indians accentuate their ethnicity though when they were resident in India, they had not been conscious of their pan-Indian or regional ethnicity. They were constantly immersed in it and so they lived it unthinkingly. However, in the new land, which is thousands of miles away from the fountainhead of Indian culture, they consciously re-enact it.

In contrast to their behaviour in America, while they visit India, NRIs advertise their links to America, and their ownership of American dollars/real estate/movable property. Ankita makes sure to wear American-bought clothes while visiting her family and friends in India. She also makes a point of showing pictures of her single family home in the San Francisco Bay Area to her friends in New Delhi. Her cousin who has settled in England uses his cell phone to send photos of his new Jeep to his family and friends back in Bangalore as soon as the car-dealer hands him the Jeep keys! And Ankita's Indian immigrant friend, also from the Bay Area, posts only 500 photos of her latest vacation in New York and Las Vegas onto her Facebook page, every one of which photos are examined minutely and commented upon by her old friends in India! In a sense, the Indian community re-invents its Indian ethnicity in America, and its American identity in India. Of course, it takes a lot of money and effort to maintain full lives in two separate nations, and only the global elite can afford to do so. Most immigrants can only aspire to such a life, but they continue trying to improve their social and economic position in both the nation of origin as well as the nation of settlement (Ong 1999).

Reproduction of Indian Culture in the Bay Area

In the San Francisco Bay Area, the cultural and material artefacts required to recreate Indianness are regularly imported from India. Some are produced in

North America and sold in Indian American retail stores, hence Indian cooking utensils, statues of Indian gods and goddesses, prayer incense sticks, Indian spices, lentils, rice, chapati flour, and frozen foods are readily available in Indian grocery stores in the US. Indian stores also sell salwar-kameez, saris, periodicals, CDs, and DVDs from the homeland. Indian immigrants bring Indian artefacts with them each time they return from a vacation to India. This easy availability of items of Indian material culture in America is a function of new technology and of economic globalization as the time and expense of transporting goods and passengers has been drastically reduced.

The spatial recreation of Indian culture in America takes place both in the Indian immigrant home, and in such special Indian locations such as the Hindu temple, the Sikh gurdwara, the Indian-Muslim mosque, the Indian-Christian church, Indian stores, restaurants, music and dance performances, movie theatres, and community centres. In the Indian home in the Bay Area, the puja room or altar, or the location of the Guru Granth Sahib, Koran or Bible, is a centre of Indianness. The pantry in the kitchen or the walk-in closet in the bedroom is often converted into a prayer room. Alternatively, a table top, or a shelf in a closet in the bedroom or living room serves as the prayer niche. Statues and photographs of Indian gods and goddesses or religious texts are set up. Incense sticks, incense stick stands, conch shells, *diyas* (lamps), prayer bells, *kumkum* (sacred red powder), scripture books, and *misri* (Indian sugar crystals offered to the gods and then consumed by the worshippers) complete the prayer paraphernalia. The kitchen is another site for reaffirmation of Indian identity. The diasporic kitchen is stocked with Indian utensils and electronic gadgets such as the *kadhai* (Indian wok), the *tava* (griddle), the *saransi* (tongs), idli (rice cake) moulds, and the electronic spice and rice grinder. Indian spices, groceries, recipe books filled with their mother's Indian recipes, and folders full of print-outs of cooking tips culled from Indian cooking sites on the internet are stacked on the shelves. Furthermore, there is usually a prayer niche dedicated to Ganesh, the Hindu god of good beginnings and prosperity. The Indian expatriate home is decorated with Indian cushion covers, bedspreads, paintings, and folk handicrafts.

The public temple is another site for the recreation of a Hindu spiritual ambience. Most Hindu temples are housed in renovated warehouses, shop fronts, or residential homes and so they do not look like temples from the outside. A few Hindu temples such as the Livermore Temple in the Bay Area are located in less expensive areas where Indians have been able to afford a large tract of land and new construction so these have been fashioned by artisans from India in accordance with the canons of Hindu temple architecture. They look like traditional Hindu temples from the inside as well as the outside: typically, there are *mandaps* (domes) and intricate ornamental moulding in the exterior and big statues and photographs of the Hindu pantheon of deities in the interior. A number of priests are usually brought on H-1 visas from India. There is daily darshan (viewing the god) and *aarti* (ritual worship with lamps) by the priest and the congregation. The temples in the Bay Area have internet sites, and priests are available for communication by email and cell phone. There are many Indian-Christian churches in the Bay Area as well as a Syrian-Christian church in Livermoore. There are also many gurdwaras in the Bay Area, of which the ones in El Sobrante and San Jose are well-known for their architectural beauty and size. Indian Muslims frequent mosques in which other South Asians worship. The Bay Area also has two Indian community centres which provide a location for elderly Indian immigrants to congregate and a site for Indian dance, music, and language classes.

In India, the passage of time is marked by puja utsavs (Hindu, Buddhist, and Jain religious festivals), eid/urz (Islamic religious festivals), Christian holy days, and secular national holidays and so Indians in the Bay Area attempt to do the same. The Indian expatriate community celebrates major annual Indian religious festivals such as Diwali, Ganapati Puja, Durga Puja, Pongal, and Guru Nanak's birth anniversary. On 15 August, India's Independence Day is also commemorated by the US resident Indians in India Day parades where movie stars are flown in from Mumbai to lead the parade, immigrant children perform music and dance shows, and local community leaders give speeches.

The Indian diasporic media is a significant source of information about current events, sports, fashions, movies, and music releases in India and in the Indian American community. News about India is easily available on the internet. At least a dozen expatriate Indian newspapers and periodicals are published in the US, including a monthly periodical called *India Currents* in the San Francisco Bay Area. Many Indian homes in the US are equipped with a dish antenna that enables the residents to view cable shows broadcast from India. The San Francisco Bay Area has a few international channels on regular American cable TV which show Indian programmes for a few hours every day. In fact, this is a common feature in all parts of the US that have a large Indian population, such as the San Francisco Bay Area, Los Angeles, New York, New Jersey, and Chicago. COMCAST cable, the mainstream cable provider in the Bay Area, provides a few Indian channels such as ZEE TV in all the counties in the Bay Area. There are also one or two radio frequencies in the Bay Area that regularly broadcast Indian talk shows and music selections in English, Hindi, and regional Indian languages. Naaz, Big Cinemas Towne 3, and AMC 6 at Mercado are the three movie theatres dedicated to showing Indian movies. Acknowledging the financial contribution of the viewership of expatriate Indians, new Bollywood movies now premiere simultaneously in Indian cities and in major Indian immigrant centres in the

West, such as London, Los Angeles, New York, and the Bay Area. Raaga and other Indian CD and DVD stores in the Bay Area stock the latest selection of Hindi and south Indian releases. The easy availability of media links to the home country makes it easy to maintain a diasporic identity, and it makes it possible to avoid adopting the local culture of the country of residence.

Drawbacks of Diasporic Identity

All cultures are continually under production and formation, hence we need to be critical of the assumption of authenticity. Questions such as 'Is the Indian culture recreated in America authentic?' and 'How can the diasporic individual aim for authenticity?' are meaningful only if we examine the various implications of the concept of cultural authenticity. As T.M. Luhrmann has said, the diasporic identity is one of the narratives that the immigrant selects in order to negotiate a space for him or herself:

Being who you purport to be, being true to yourself, being genuine, seems—on the surface, at least—to be more difficult in a world in which one's nationality is not obvious, one's historical past cannot be assumed, and one's ambitions and hopes and achievable goals cannot be read from one's surroundings. (1996: 200)

Like all diasporic cultures, Indian diasporic culture is derivative by nature. However, it is authentic in the sense that it speaks the truth of the aspirations of the immigrant community. Naturally, it is impossible for Indians in America to exactly replicate the living, and constantly evolving, culture in India. What they produce in the name of Indian culture is authentic only in so far as it responds to immigrant needs. Indian culture as experienced in the US is the mass culture of the Indian diaspora, embodied by popular Bollywood stars performing huge live shows in America, convenient ready-to-wear Indian fashions in synthetic silks that appeal to NRI tastes, and religious rituals commonly observed by the Indian immigrant community. The last includes remote darshan and puja (electronic worship for a fee, available on the internet web pages set up by specific temples in India), Ganesh puja (commonly performed by local Hindu priests before opening a new business enterprise), *Griha Pravesh* puja (puja to bless a new house), Vahan puja (puja to bless a new car), *namkaran* (christening a newborn baby), and *annaprasanam* (blessing the first solid food consumed by an infant).

Expatriate attempts to replicate 'high' Indian culture, such as with performances of Indian classical dance and music, and the works of renaissance regional poets, playwrights, and choreographers are patronized by only a small minority of the diasporic population. Whether 'high' or 'low' Indian culture, the community leaders, artists, cultural trainers, and parents of children who perform in Indian cultural productions often discuss how the actively learning and performing Indian arts serve to anchor immigrants to their cultural heritage. Indian culture is seen to be intricately woven with Indians value-systems and moral norms. Kapila justifies the time and money she has spent on her daughter's Bharatnatyam training and *arangetram* by emphasizing how her daughter has become familiar with the stories about Hindu Gods and Goddesses through her dancing lessons: 'My daughter's dance teacher explains the stories behind the songs the class dances with, and so at least my daughter now knows many stories about Krishna, Radha, and also about the Dashavatara'. Sucheta Mazumdar argues that there is a hidden agenda in the reproduction of Indian culture in the American diaspora. It is to prove the moral superiority of ethnics over Westerners, and to keep American-raised offspring from rebelling against the older generation of Indian immigrants (1996). I am in agreement with Mazumdar, I believe that the obsession with perpetuating a diasporic Indian identity is sometimes caused by a misguided desire to turn majoritarian superiority on its head, and to claim moral and cultural superiority over the Caucasian mainstream.

In 2006, the controversy about the California middle school social studies textbook is an example of divisions within the Indian community about how to represent itself in the US. The state of California revises its textbooks every six years. It welcomes suggestions from the public in this effort. In 2006, two separate self-appointed entities called the Vedic Foundation and the Hindu Educational Foundation, suggested edits to the textbooks. They claimed their objective was to soften the emphasis on inequitable or disreputable Hindu practices such as caste, sati, and polytheism in the textbooks. However, Indian immigrant secular groups such as Friends of South Asia and Coalition Against Communalism, as well as scholars of Hinduism such as Harvard Sanskrit Professor Michael Witzel, and renowned historian Professor Stanley Wolpert, protested against the revisions suggested by the two Foundations. They explained that these revisions erased past and contemporary histories of oppression for the sake of a falsely positive portrayal of Hinduism. In the end, the Board of Education accepted only a few of the suggested revisions of the Hindu groups (*San Francisco Chronicle*, 28 February 2006).

Despite the patent lack of authenticity of Indian culture (re)produced in America, most of the Indian immigrants I interviewed feel that their diasporic identity is the only one which they can use to their advantage. In emphasizing an American identity, many Indians suspect that they would be taking up a place in America only as a model minority, or as (inferior) Brown people; these are positions they are unwilling to assume.

Class Status

The few thousand Indian immigrants who came to the US before the 1965 Immigration Act were mostly from agricultural communities in northern

India. They worked in the lumber industry, in railroad construction, and in farming. By the middle of the last century, most of the first wave of immigrant Indians had settled in central California, had bought or leased land, and had become farmers.

The Immigration Act of 1965 opened the US borders to an inflow from nations that had previously been banned from sending immigrants. The provisions of the Act of 1965 explicitly stated that only Indians with professional qualifications would be allowed to immigrate to the US but their families were also allowed entry. The post-1965 wave of Indian immigrants was therefore highly educated and well qualified. Both economic and occupational indicators show that the second wave of Indian immigrants in the US have been extremely successful. However, once the post-1965 wave of immigrants became US citizens, they began to bring in non-professional family members who were not very successful in America. They opened gas stations, convenience stores, and motels, became cab drivers, nannies, and cooks but still found it hard to make ends meet. As Madhulika Khandelwal has written, there is a significant number of Indians who live in dire poverty in America, but they are not acknowledged by the American Indian community as their own (2002). However, on the whole, Indian Americans are still a model minority. According to the 2008 Census, 68 per cent of Asian Indians 25 and older in the US had a bachelor's degree or more education, and 36 per cent had a graduate or professional degree. Naturally, these excellent qualifications led to well-remunerated employment; in addition, many Asian Indians in the US also owned their own businesses (US Census Documents, <www.census.gov>). According to the 2004 Census, 61 per cent of Asian Indians workers were in management, professional, and related occupations (US Census Documents, <www.census.gov>). The 2000 US Census showed that Indian Americans had among the highest income per centile in the country and that the median household income was $60,093, about 155 per cent of the national average (2000 US Census Documents, <www.census.gov>). As professional Indian working women in the Bay Area, most of my interviewees strongly emphasized their substantial incomes and real estate holdings in order to indicate a superior class position.

Many of the more successful women I interviewed were in middle management positions in American corporations. While they were proud of how far they had come, none of them had risen above mid-level management, unless they owned their own business. I also noticed that many of these women occupied mediatory positions. For example, Aparajita worked as a shop floor manager for many years, mediating between the senior management of the shop and the sales persons, stockroom workers, and janitorial staff. Her present position of human resources manager means that she also performs mediatory functions to ease communication between junior and senior employees in the company. Smita occupies a similar mediatory niche. She is an outsourcing software production manager and her job is to communicate the requirements of the senior management of her company to the software developers located in India and so she shuttles back and forth between the company headquarters in San Francisco and the software writers in Mumbai. Lakshmi is a manager in the manufacturing department of a Bay Area biopharmaceutical corporation. She mediates between the Vice President of Scientific Development and the laboratory technicians, many of whom are from racial minorities.

The experience of colonialism has had a lasting effect on the abilities and conditioning of Asian Indian immigrants seeking employment. Even first generation Indian immigrants usually possess good English reading, writing, and speaking skills, but many other first generation immigrant Asians and Hispanics, who were not colonized by the British colonial domination, are not proficient in English. This puts them at a disadvantage vis-à-vis Indian job seekers for management positions.

As discussed in this chapter, in colonial India, Western-educated Indians formed a colonial middle class that was subordinate to the British and superior to the Indian masses. They supervised the working poor and also oversaw the execution of the orders of colonial masters by the Indian labour force. In the post-colonial situation, the progeny of the Western-educated bourgeoisie led the 'brain drain' which is the emigration of highly educated and professionally qualified youths who could not find appropriate opportunities in higher education or suitable employment in India. Historically trained to act as mediators between the ruling class and the masses, the Westernized Indian bourgeoisie re-enacts its mediatory role in its new country of residence.

Kamala Visweswaran writes:

A prior historical experience of structural position as a middle term may lend itself to the anticipation of a middle position in new contexts. It is precisely the mediatory ability, that active negotiation of invitation and exclusion, that has made possible the community's flexible insertion into US race relations, making it diasporic by design. (1997: 17–18)

Visweswaran has identified the colonial historical roots of the Indian American immigrant middleman minority position. None of my subjects explicitly articulated awareness of the strategic usefulness of their ancestors' experience of mediating between the managerial class and the workers in colonial India. However, many subjects did make a point of letting me know that their father had been in a managerial position in India. They also emphasized that they were from Western-educated, progressive, liberal, elite or upper-middle class families in India. Such families are typically part of the 'babu' class of knowledge workers who managed colonial interests, and now manage post-colonial industries and the state administration.

These mediatory positions do not provide adequate security to Indian expatriates however, so they therefore reactivate ethnicity in order to bolster their self and identity. Focusing on the ethnic distinctiveness of the community serves two purposes. First, Indians in the US can set themselves apart from Blacks and Hispanics, two groups that first generation Indian immigrants would like to outdo economically and they can also avoid miscegenation. Second, the Indian colonial and diasporic history of mediation between separate races is emphasized each time they remind the American public of the ethnic heritage of Indians in the US.

Two Identities, Two Selves

The long duration immigrants I interviewed and interacted with, displayed remarkable speed in moving between the two persona of Indian and American, as and when the situation required. They undertook both performances with gusto to the point that these individuals seem both more American and more Indian than any of the other persons I interacted with. As previously mentioned the great length of duration of residence in the US has made this group acutely aware of the intricacies of American social, political, financial, and cultural life. However, over the years, long duration immigrants find themselves becoming increasingly conscious of their 'brownness', and of how Brown people are often shut out of positions of influence and power in the West. Hence, these immigrants attempt to project an ethnic and diasporic persona in order to dispute the idea of their 'brownness'. Diasporic identity is enhanced by the reproduction of Indian culture in the US. Rather than skin colour, the moral values, educational qualifications, historical heritage, language, food, ancient performative arts, and the purported economic success of the community are highlighted. Moreover, it would not be wrong to hypothesize that the invocation of Indian moral norms is meant to challenge the idea of Caucasian superiority. Another reason for showcasing diasporic identity is that it accentuates the long Indian history of have of being favoured middlemen minority collaborators with White powers in both colonial as well as post-colonial diasporic multiracial formations. Re-activation of Indianness is also meant to impress an Indian identity upon the minds of expatriate children and youths.

Self and identity are shaped by interactions between the individual and the surrounding social milieu. In the 1930s, C.H. Cooley and G.H. Mead argued that human society is marked by the necessity for learning the symbolic or conventional meanings of words and actions. These are learned through social contact communicated through symbolic interaction, that is, by visualizing oneself in the same manner that others would. Shared symbolic systems are needed for role playing as it is only possible to learn to play role because individuals can take on the roles of others. George Herbert Mead identifies two stages in the development of the self. First comes 'I', that is, the inner, unpremeditated, and subjective self, and then comes 'Me', which reflects upon symbolic and role assigned communication with others, and which is then able to incorporate societal values into the self-concept (1934).

Mead outlined a separation between 'I' and 'Me' (ibid.). My understanding is that the 'I' of first generation Indian working women long-settled in the US remains largely Indian, but is decidedly American in certain moral values, tastes in food, clothing, and leisure activity preferences. The 'Me' is transformed to a transnational/diasporic/*pravasi* 'Me', because the long duration working female immigrant is constantly poised between radically different cultures. The longer the work experience in America, the greater the capacity for presentation of a repertoire of behaviours that conform to expectations prevailing in the workplace, and in other American contexts. The inner self continues to be somewhat Indian, even while it is gradually influenced by American mores. Moreover, expatriate Indian women who have lived and worked in the US for a long time return to Indian choices in a few key aspects of their lives for the sake of building up self-respect and an adequate identity. Indian immigrant home life retains its ethnic flavour not simply because of the links to an Indian past, but also due to constant reaffirmation and active Indianization in the present. Indianization is initiated by those very women who are adept at projecting an American self when the situation demands it. This recursive pattern of reproducing Indianness in America arises out of a need to reinforce a sense of self-adequacy, and is not perceived to be in contradiction to an American identity (Steele 1988). In fact due to various macro politico-economic factors, Indians in the US believe that a strategic (and partial) return to their ethnicity will help them to rise within class/race formations within the US.

While I did find a contrast in the 'for presentation to Indians' roles, identities, and selves, and the 'for presentation to mainstream Americans' roles, identities, and selves in the lives of the women I interviewed and observed, I found that the longer they have been in the US, and more specifically, the longer they have been in the American workforce, the more adept they become at switching back and forth between the two identities. In fact, they often cross over from one identity to another, both at work and at home.

SETTLED IMMIGRANT NON-WORKING WOMEN: IN A TIME WARP

Comparative analysis searches for variance in experience across different groups so while my study mainly focuses on Indian working women in the

US, I also interviewed a number of settled non-working US resident Indian women in the Bay Area. My purpose was to find out the differences, or lack thereof, made by participation in the American workplace. On the whole, it seems that immigrant non-working Indian women in the US exhibit a very low degree of Americanization. Confinement to their home and to the Indian expatriate community has resulted in effective insulation from American society. The media, local services (such as stores, physicians, banks), and the children of these women were their only link to American ideas, customs, behaviour, morals, law, art, and belief systems. In most cases, the husbands of non-working expatriate Indian women did not encourage the Americanization of their wives or children.

To my surprise, I found that settled Indian immigrant non-working women were not only less Americanized than any of my other respondents, but they also exhibited a lower degree of identification with current Indian thought and practice than any of my other interviewees. What they seemed most comfortable with was the culture of the India of the 1960s, 1970s, and 1980s, that is, the India they had emigrated from. In a sense, these women lived in a time warp. Despite their frequent visits to India, their behaviour and modes of thinking were frozen in the cultural habits of the India of many decades ago. In America, they formed close-knit communities with other settled Indian immigrants and most of their friends were other non-working Indian women who had settled in the US along with their families.

To give a few examples, Kusum says:

I love to visit India, I visit India often, but I usually end up feeling out of place there too. I don't relate to my school and college friends anymore. I wear *saris* and salwar kameezes, they wear pants, shirts, jeans, or the new kurtis and micro-mini salwar kameezes that are the latest fashion there. I chat about the latest achievements of my children, they tell me about their own achievements at work. Most of them have flourishing careers in India. I am not employed.

Arunima says:

Because my children are growing up in the US, I am very particular about speaking to my children in Bengali, and making sure they reply in Bengali. But when I visit Kolkata, I find that all their cousins, that is, my nieces and nephews, constantly chatter with each other in English, not Bengali!

Parvati says:

You know how I have problems with American culture. I hate the sex and violence shown on American TV, the emphasis on dating, and the drugs in American junior high and high school. But despite all these bad influences, I think I have been able to bring up my daughter very well. She listens to me. She goes to school only to study there, she doesn't waste too much of time on socializing. My husband and I don't even allow her to go the mall on her own or with her friends. But look at the young people in India nowadays. What strange clothes they wear, all MTV type clothes! They start dating in high school! And when they grow up, they don't want to be doctors, engineers or teachers any more, they all want to be fashion models or beauty queens! They grew up in India, but what Indian culture have they learned?! My Moni was raised in America, but she is more Indian than them!

Working immigrant women are constantly exposed to the American 'other' at work, hence they become increasingly capable of playing the role that the American co-worker expects of them, that of an American employee and workplace colleague. This also helps them to perform expected roles in non-work situations in America, such as at the store, the doctor's clinic, the child's school, sport events, movie theatres, etc. This transforms their 'Me' from completely Indian to significantly American.

In the case of non-working Indian women, there is very little Americanization of the 'Me'. Deprived of the opportunity to interact with Americans, Indian immigrant women who do not work outside the home fail to observe or learn general attitudes and behavioural characteristics prevalent in American society. The 'Me' of such women is reflective of the community in the midst of which they spend maximum time and in which they are most comfortable, that of the Indian immigrant community. Within this community, they usually limit their interaction to other non-working Indian women resident in the US with their families. Communication within this highly integrated community is frequent and thorough, including daily phone calls or emails, weekly lunch or dinner get-togethers, social exchanges at weekly classes in which immigrant children are taught Indian dance, music, language, or religious texts, and monthly meetings at Indian regional and religious festivals at the Hindu temple.

Having shown the seclusion of non-working Indian immigrant women from mainstream American society, we can understand how unlikely it is that the 'Me' of such women will adopt societal values and self-conceptions that conform to American expectations. The high density of communication with fellow-Indian immigrants insulates their 'Me' from growing American. Since both are based on Indian values and norms, there is abundant harmony between their inner, unpremeditated, and subjective 'I', and their conceptual 'Me' which reflects upon symbolic and role assigned communication with others. Hence, though they might suffer from numerous socio-economic disadvantages that result from being cut off from the prevalent American social milieu, immigration related social adjustment struggles cause fewer instances of psychological dissonance in the selves of home-bound non-working Indian immigrant women.

TOWARDS GENERALIZATION: THE CONSTRUCTION OF THE SELF

In my study of the self and identity of Indian immigrant women employed in the San Francisco-Oakland-San Jose Area, I have used analytical tools from various areas of study such as cultural anthropology, social psychology, gender studies, and ethnic studies. Post-colonial analysis and the recent literature on globalization have also been of enormous assistance to me. I have mapped the exact manner in which labour-force participation and the length of residence in the US intersect in their effect on the construction of self-conception by middle class Indian women living and working in the San Francisco Bay Area. I am hopeful that my research results are a worthy contribution to the general analysts of the current scenario of accelerated regional, intra-national, and international migration across the globe.

Being Brown in America, Indians have secured a mediatory niche for themselves in American race and class formations. Predisposed to middlemanship by their colonial history of mediating between White colonial powers and the native labouring masses of India, post-colonial Indian bourgeoisie who migrate to the US act as a middleman minority. They facilitate the execution of the directives of a mostly White managerial class by a working class composed of some Whites, as well as Blacks, Hispanics, and Asians.

While the social and financial security achieved by a mediatory position is quite gratifying, Indian immigrants in the US are not satisfied with it. They would like to be something more than conveniently positioned 'Brown people'. Also, being racially prejudiced themselves, they would like to distinguish themselves from other people of colour such as Hispanics and Blacks. A re-composition of Indian ethnicity provides a suitable vehicle to fulfil such yearnings. Indian ethnicity provides a convenient hook on which to hang one's identity. A return to India ethnicity bolsters self and identity, and this is not perceived to contradict the formation of an American identity. Indians in the US feel that a strategic (though partial) re-activation of Indian ethnicity will help them to rise in the race/class hierarchy in the US and provide them with an upwardly mobile American identity. Misguided by chauvinistic notions of ethnic pride, displays of Indian ethnicity are also meant to show that Indian spirituality, family oriented Indian values, superior Indian moral standards, higher levels of Indian educational and economic success, and a glorious ancient Indian historical heritage are indicators of the general superiority of Indians over all other American races and ethnicities. In the main, this is a sadly misguided attempt to improve the position of Indians in America.

Resurrection of Indian ethnicity also provides a path to the establishment of an Indian global diasporic identity. There are Indian immigrants all over the world, for Indian immigration began with the export of Indian indentured labourers to African, West Indian, and other remotely located plantations in colonial times, and has continued in the post-colonial era in the 'brain-drain' of highly qualified Indian technical professionals and students to the West, and the outflow of Indian white and blue-collar workers to the oil-rich nations of the Arabian Gulf. A few Indians have earned phenomenal fame and riches outside India. Millions of desi immigrants across the globe attempt to make the achievements of these few spectacularly successful Indians abroad a part of their own identity by projecting a 'global Indian' self in their dealings with the natives of the lands they have settled in. Indian transnational networks shape income-generating projects, marital alliances, and artistic fusion across several distant continents and oceans. In the overseas situation, local and global connections of the Indian regional level flourish just as vibrantly, if not more so than pan-Indian global networks. In the Bay Area, events organized by local chapters of pan-Indian American associations such as the Federation of Indian in America (FIA) are sparsely attended, but local Indian regional associations such as those of the Punjabis, Tamils, Telugus, Bengalis, and Marathis are very popular. Regional Indian congeries also have effective global systems. Gujarati and Sindhi global loyalties have translated into transnational import-export enterprises and Patel-Motel chains across entire continents. Tamil, Telugu, and Andhraite regional collaborations across the world have led to technological globe-spanning businesses, such as outsourcing computer software programming from Western locales to Bangalore and Hyderabad. Bengali sitar maestros resident in the US play with fellow-Bengali tabla players settled in the UK and produce 'world music'. These are a few of the innumerable current examples of Indian regional socio-economic networks that function at the global level. Presentation of the ethnic self in the country of settlement is intimately linked with the desire to benefit from transnational pan-Indian or Indian regional ties across the globe.

Despite the projection of Indianness, American cultural competence continues to be a requirement of professional and personal survival and success in the US. I discovered that the self of Indian expatriate women who have lived and worked in the US for long is both very 'American' and very 'Indian'. Their high degree of Americanization is due to long and thorough interaction with 'mainstream' Americans. In fact Indian women in the American workplace feel the need to prove their cultural competence by fitting in with their American co-workers. At the same time, their pervasive Indianness is due to reproduction of diasporic Indian ethnicity in specific aspects of life in order to build up self-esteem. Post-migration self-esteem diminishes upon perception of one's 'racial minority and hence non-elite' status in America, whereas re-evocation of ethnicity appeals to several Indian women as a means to boost self-esteem. Though both 'American' and 'Indian', Indian professional women are often evaluated as not American enough at work and inadequately Indian at home. Though they are easily hired and promoted for technical positions, due to a widely held perception that Indians lack communicative skills, they are rejected in positions requiring interpersonal skills and managerial abilities. Also, Indian women are trained to be modest and accommodating, hence they are at a disadvantage in the American corporate environment where the commonly accepted work ethic favours self-promotion and self-assertion. At the same time, traditional men and women within the immigrant community often criticize 'modern' Indian women in America for their forthright and aggressive behaviour as it is deemed not fitting for Indian women.

Being largely confined to the home, non-working expatriate Indian women are effectively insulated from American society. Hence, their level of Americanization is low. Surprisingly, such women exhibit very little identification with the culture and values of present-day India and the majority of these subjects live in a time warp. They still function according to the culture of the India they emigrated from two to three decades ago. America-resident Indian women who are employed have greater agency than their non-working counterparts, for despite their residence in the progressive environment of the US, the traditional Indian patriarchal bias continues to be extremely active in the lives of Indian housewives in the US. The absence of extended family in the country of settlement allows greater opportunity for companionship between immigrant married couples and more chances for married women to act independently. Yet, newfound privacy and the absence of mediating family seniors in America also heightens the peril of domestic abuse and wife beating when things go wrong in an immigrant marriage. Indian women in the US, especially those who are not employed, do not know how to go about seeking help from the administrative and health care systems in the US.

Concluding comments: Indianness versus Americanness

In this chapter I have used some of the analytical concepts of self and identity formulated by diasporic theorists, as well as symbolic interactionists such as George Herbert Mead and Irving Goffman to examine the degree of Indianness versus Americanness in professional immigrant Indian women in the San Francisco Bay Area.

I have differentiated between Indian expatriate women in the Bay Area on the basis of variables such as length of residence in the US and duration of employment in the American workplace. While I have mainly focused on working women in the Indian community, I have also studied a small group of non-working women for the sake of comparison.

The self of Indian expatriate women who have lived and worked in the US for long is both very American and very Indian. The high degree of Americanness is due to long and thorough interaction with mainstream Americans. The great extent of Indianness is due to reproduction of diasporic Indian ethnicity in specific aspects of life in order to build up self-esteem. A major part of the immigrant adjustment process involves readjusting one's sense of self. An Indian professional who might have been unemployed or underemployed in India, might nevertheless have been part of the social elite in India on account of his or her high caste, extensive family connections, or high level of education. Due to his or her technical qualifications, such a person might have no problem finding employment in the US, but after prolonged interaction with mainstream Americans, he or she may suffer from low-esteem due to a belief that as a Brown person, he or she has no hope of becoming a part of the social or political elite in the US. While this is a common complaint in the Indian immigrant community, the truth is that due to the great wealth they have amassed, or due to the political connections they have nurtured over the years, or due to their brilliant academic achievements, many Indians in the US have in fact been successful in penetrating American elite circles.

Symbolic interactionism is a conception of the human world which holds that people use symbols to interact with each other and with the environment to fulfil their needs. Human beings use symbols to give meaning to their world and the assignment of symbols to specific objects makes social interaction possible. Social interplay enables individuals and groups to construct a specific reality. Though social reality is an artificial construct due to the phenomenon of reification, human beings usually regard their social order as prior, immutable, inevitable, and necessary.

Humans treat themselves as part of their objective environment. The self is created through interaction between the individual and society by means of collectively ratified symbols. The self is therefore socially produced in that an individual can only be what socially available symbols allow him to be. The individual's personal qualities, capabilities, and intentions are shaped by, and reflected in, socially available symbols. However, the self is also individually created because human conduct is the result of the interplay between individual spontaneous subjective impulse and objective reflection about one's spontaneous response to a situation.

The 'Me' directs individuals to take on the role of others towards themselves in order to tailor their behaviour to social expectations. Once the 'Me' has performed its role, the 'I' comes back into action. The 'I' and 'Me' are phases of alternating consciousness, thus human action is self-referential, for the self comprises a crucial part of every individual's environment. Human action is also decided by the expected reactions of significant reference groups with which the individual interacts.

We have seen that the expectation of others is crucial in deciding behaviour by the self, yet human behaviour is not perfectly predictable. This is partly because no individual is the same in the eyes of all others, hence the expectations of different people are varied.

The individual changes their self in each case in order to fit the expectations generated by the role of others. Thus an individual might develop contradictory self-conceptions (identity, self-image, and self-esteem) which make it difficult to accurately predict conduct. Another factor that causes unpredictability is that human impulse cannot always be brought under control by socialized self-reference.

Using the tools offered by symbolic interactionism, my research goals have included analysis of the 'I'-'Me' phase function in my subjects, identification of divergent role expectations, and a resolution (or not) of contradictory self-conceptions. The inner 'I' of long duration immigrants is no longer fully Indian, as due to prolonged American influences, it is significantly American. The outer 'Me' is diasporic in that it constantly alternates between newly learned, but well rehearsed, American roles and so-called traditional Indian ethnic roles.

CHAPTER V

Conclusion

THIS WORK HAS been an exploration of the forging of selves and identities of Asian Indian working women, mainly professional and semi-professional, in the San Francisco-Oakland Bay Area. Such an endeavour may be considered worthwhile for several reasons. Arguably, anthropologists today must be cognizant of such sweeping changes in global populations in the current era of late capitalism. Traditionally a study of the other in the colonial and capitalist periphery, anthropology must now adjust to the entrance of the other in unprecedented numbers into the Western world. The self of the global metropolis and the other are in closer proximity than ever before, and the discipline of anthropology must record and analyse the intermingling of the two in the 'brave new world' of incessant cultural and racial hybridity and the era of far-reaching technological and financial liaisons across national and ethnic boundaries.

Second, from a theoretical point of view, there are some interesting issues in the problematic of studying the construction of Asian Indian women's selves and identities in the US. Globalization has brought about flows of finance, technology, goods, people, and ideas across the globe in unprecedented volumes. Capitalism from its inception in the North Atlantic seaboard brought about increasing global exchanges. Now in its advanced stage, capitalism has compressed time and space so radically that we can no longer assume the isomorphism of the nation and its citizens anymore (Gupta and Ferguson 1997). This has created, as Arjun Appadurai (1996) has argued in his work on the cultural dimensions of globalization, cosmopolitan and diasporic identities that consist of disjunctive components. In light of this, this work attempts to analyse the construction of selfhood by women who have been able to immigrate to the US due to neoliberal immigration policies approved by the American state in the mid-1960s. I have analysed the making of self and identity of professional working women in the Asian Indian diaspora in the Silicon Valley in this context.

Third, it may be very worthwhile to notice the salient presence of the Asian Indian professionals in US from a pragmatic point of view. There are 1.7 million Indians in the US, many of whom work in the Silicon Valley. Approximately half of the Asian Indian women in America work, and of these, a significant number live and work in the Bay Area and the Silicon Valley. These women are a worthy subject of study for they form a substantial proportion of the technical workers in the informatics industry. The fundamental question of this study has been: how do they construct a self and identity that is adequate to negotiate the racialization and sexism perceived to be features of the workplace in the US, and the gender bias and parochialism found at home? Needless to say, as well as the issues mentioned above, from the vantage point of contemporary research in gender studies such a study is worthwhile.

The establishment of Indian immigrant communities in North America commenced with the arrival of north Indian labourers in the lumber mills and railway construction sites in Canada and US in the late nineteenth century. The trajectory of developments since then has been outlined in Chapter I, along with a brief discussion of the theoretical approaches relevant to the problems developed in this work. The work then moves on to construct a theoretical model of the various stages of female Asian Indian diasporic identity formation in the Silicon Valley.

I conducted extensive interviews with Asian Indian professional working women in the Silicon Valley, and so there are in the preceding pages, lengthy first person narratives by my subjects, for I considered it useful to allow the women to speak in their own voice. As I have shown, my interviewees displayed contested identities in which the performance of American assimilationism conflicted with that of diasporic Indian ethnicism. Undoubtedly the level of assimilation or accommodation vis-à-vis mainstream American society increases with length of residence and employment history in the US, but parallel to that there is an increasing emphasis on Indian diasporic identity among those who have a long residence experience and employment history. It has been argued in this study that the following model explains how these conflicting trends develop in the self and identity of Asian Indian women in white-collar professions in the Silicon Valley.

In the first stage of identity formation, in the first couple of years in the US, my subjects dealt with the shock of arrival in America. Due to the pervasiveness of Western culture in ex-colonial India, my subjects had imagined that they were adequately familiar with Western culture to negotiate the intricacies of daily life and culture in America. Yet, when they got off the plane from India, they found that their ignorance of local linguistic accents, currency, cuisine, fashions, traffic regulations, and modes of behaviour, were sufficiently alienating in the US to cause them great discomfiture.

In the second stage, my subjects became increasingly familiar with American ways of being. After a couple of years of residence and employment in the US, Indian immigrant women became adept at 'being American'. They were as comfortable with American linguistic nuances, behavioural codes, cuisine, apparel, and leisure time activities as they were with Indian equivalents. This made it easier for them to 'fit in' while interacting with Americans in the workplace, and also in non-work situations. In this stage, the women completely identified with the host population.

In the third stage, immigrant residents in the US for more than a decade, having had prolonged interaction with 'mainstream' Americans, appear to be sceptical of effective assimilation. They voice a belief that irrespective of age, occupation, financial status, or general abilities, individuals of Asian Indian origin are primarily viewed by 'mainstream' Americans as 'racial minority immigrants', or at best, as a 'model minority'. My subjects conveyed to me that they would like to be something more than a conveniently employable 'model minority', that such a characterization is racialized and make Asians part of the 'inassimilable' minorities in the US, and that they feel they will be perceived as an ethnic minority for the foreseeable future. As Espiritu has said, by practicing selective inclusion, the dominant majority includes racial and ethnic minorities in spaces where there is an economic need for them, but not in social contexts. Also, being racially chauvinistic themselves, Asian Indians would like to distinguish themselves from other ethnic and racial minorities such as Hispanics and Blacks.

In this stage, Asian Indian women in the US became acutely aware of being 'misrecognized' as 'Brown immigrants' by 'mainstream' Americans. In some other contexts 'misrecognition' has been the unexpected result of the faithful 'mimicry' of the ruling race by the ruled ethnicities (Bhabha 1994). In the US, most of my subjects identified with the Whites, but the mainstream, in the immigrants' perception, did not accept them. Due to my subjects' conviction that Americans saw them mainly as Indian immigrants, they embraced the role of ethnic representatives of India. Thus, the womens' emphatic identification with the Asian Indian minority is caused by the perception of native-born Americans that Asian Indian women are not regular Americans, but rather, that they are stereotypical Indian immigrant women. As Espiritu (1997) also pointed out, Asian women often become what the dominant majority perceives them to be. Of course, there are other reasons too for the attachment to Indianness: it is an old habit, a source of comfort, a long held identity, and a link to older and younger generations.

Indian ethnicity provides a convenient marker of one's identity. And hence, returning to Indian ethnicity props up the self and identity. Interestingly, this is not seen to detract from the formation of an American identity. Indian immigrants in the US seem to believe that a planned partial reactivation of Indian ethnicity will assist them in climbing up the race/class hierarchies of the US, and will also enable them to retain their 'model minority' position. The underlying *leitmotif* of the reproduction of Indian ethnicity by immigrants who have settled outside the borders of India is the repeated emphasis on the supposed superiority of Indian spirituality, moral standards, and historical heritage. Other observers have also noted that non-White ethnic groups use the discourse of moral superiority to transform negative ascription into positive affirmation. Despite the reaffirmation of Indian diasporic identity, American cultural competence continues to be a requirement for professional and personal survival and success in the US. At the same time, Indian diasporic women are expected to be the bearers of ethnic culture in the immigrant community (Sucheta Mazumdar 1996; Shamita Dasgupta 1998; Priya Agarwal 1991), particularly as mothers who should transmit Indian culture to their children.

Arguably, the above explanation of the reassertion of ethnicity may enable us to understand the immigrants' dilemma and the complexities of assimilation on which much has been written from the 1960s to more recent theoretical interventions. From the vantage point of the woman immigrant, in this instance the Asian Indian, certain new perspectives emerge, aside from the perspective of reclamation of ethnic identities from the late 1960s through certain movements in the public sphere concerned with civil rights and/or cultural autonomy and the agency of native Indians, Chicanos, Asians, etc.

My belief is that in the first two years of residence and work experience in the US, my subjects seemed to undergo an identity crisis. The ego identity of individual personality is based on group identity and social heritage. The group and social environment changes radically when new immigrants first enter a new country, and they become especially conscious of this change when they interact with local people at work. Due to the shock of acculturation and Americanization, including the pull of ethnic (and initially, national) consciousness, my subjects all experienced a climactic psychological change. Despite the continuity of inner identity, a perception exists that many, if not most, former social habits, skills, behaviour and values are irrelevant in the new situation. The resultant struggle to rapidly adopt locally accepted customs, moral standards, and skills causes an internal strife that appears to be resolved as a function of the time that it takes to adjust to the new environment.

The conflicting demands of the roles of career-oriented woman in the American workforce on one hand, and that of the traditional Indian housewife on the other, create considerable dissonance in the psyche of Asian Indian immigrant women.

The second stage is when the psychological advantages of becoming a part of the American workforce begin to appear: first, Asian Indian women who are employed outside their home find more opportunities to acculturate into the American mainstream, and second, idealization of gender-equity at the workplace helps the women to form an independent identity. Of course, there might not be actual equality between men and women at the place of employment, but even the rhetoric of equal rights for all has an impact on the women. The tendency to be 'Indian at home and as American as possible in the workplace context' asserts itself.

Indianness at home tends to mean a return to the inequitable patriarchal relations that characterize the traditional Indian family. This inequity at home is difficult to accept for Indian immigrant women who aspire to be treated equals in their place of work.

In the third stage, increased exposure to non-Indians in the workplace hastens the realization that Asian Indian immigrants are unlikely to be completely accepted as 'one of us' by Americans. Rosemary Marangoly George criticizes immigrant writers who promote assimilation as a primary immigrant ambition, for such writers overlook the fact that for ethnic minorities in the US, assimilation into the mainstream is possible only as a minority (1998). Such a minority identity has to be reconciled with the workplace requirement of Americanness.

All of these contradictory demands on the self, create a conflicted, dissonance-ridden self. It has been argued that all comprehensive models of the self, contain a self-system that functions to 'sustain phenomenal experience images of the self, past, present, and future as having adaptive and moral adequacy'; the goal of the self-system is to 'maintain global conceptions of self-adequacy' and people eliminate the effect of specific self-threats by 'affirming central, valued, aspects of the self' (Steele 1988: 289). On account of the conflicting demands on their self created by the situation the immigrant Asian Indian working women find themselves in, particularly in the stage when they have had long residence and work experience in US, they need to respond to such threats to their self-integrity and the internal dissonance by various means, including the reaffirmation of Indian ethnicity.

While the above set of arguments constitutes the major thesis of this volume and is mooted in Chapter I and elaborated in different chapters throughout this work, Chapter II is focused upon the motivations and experiences of the immigrant Asian Indian women who are active in the American workplace. The testimonies of the women interviewed show clearly that while both psychological and social motivations important, the predominant motivation is economic. The increase in work participation by women as a general trend in recent times in the US has been explained (England 1992) in terms of the growth in the numbers of single women, an unprecedented growth in the service sector, and the need for a double income in a family where one partner may be unemployed or under-employed due to the recent recessions. The first explanation is not very relevant so far as Asian Indians are concerned since there are few single permanent migrant females, and the divorce rate is low. The other two factors however are pertinent: most of the subjects are in the service sector, and so a double income is desired both as an insurance against the failure of one income and also to enable access to higher living standards. My Indian American interviewees were frank about the importance of a supplemental female income.

As Stier (1991) has argued, it is not economic pressure alone but the family context and background which matter to women entering the workplace. There is, for example, a pressure of expectation: the level of education is well above average in the Asian Indian community in the US (Ortiz 1994), expected productivity in the labour market is high, and the parental background of immigrants is favourable to engagement in skilled or professional work. As I have shown, work participation of women 'back home' in India is also high. According to the 1991 Indian Census, the national average is 35.9 per cent in the 15 to 59 age group, and even higher at 43.6 per cent in rural India. My interviews conducted in India indicated favourable opinion towards working women in the middle classes, to which class the immigrants generally belong, so the desire to find work and enhance family income seems pervasive in India as much as in the US. However, in comparison to the Indian community in the US, in India there was a lower level of acknowledgement of the importance of a secondary female income.

Expectations are connected with status enhancement as well. Brenner's arguments (1998) with respect to the women's role in Javanese society regarding the production and conservation of wealth, and the transformation of it into cultural objects for the enhancement of family status, are also applicable to the Indian American community. The pattern is the same in the case of the Chinese immigrants as depicted by Aihwa Ong (1999) who shows that a major ambition among these immigrants is to convert economic capital into prestige capital in the new land as much as in the former country of residence. In the age of consumerism, the acquisition of material objects is also the highway to status enhancement. However, as well as high consumption and acquisition, my subjects, particularly the non-working Indian women in the US, also mentioned the educational achievements of children and participation in Indian cultural activities, as further paths to status.

The most important consequence of working and earning, and therefore an implicit motivation for Asian Indian women to be active in the workplace, is the agency that it brings to the woman in the family. As in the case of some other Asians (such as Filipinos) in the US (Espiritu 1997, 2003), in the Asian Indian family, the woman who earns a salary also acquires the power to make decisions. Secondly, according to the subjects interviewed, the fact that the working woman is exposed to the idea of gender equality in American culture and in the workplace means that the hold of patriarchal values in the family begins to loosen. Moreover, access to the process of acculturation in the

American world is itself a potentially liberating experience. The extent to which that potential is realized would depend, of course, on the particularities of family context and cultural practices of the segment of Indian society it belongs to. In conservative Indian points of view, there is a prejudice against the career woman, of which the analogous concept of the *wanita karier* in Indonesia is analysed in Brenner (1998). The interviewees did not emphasize this as an impediment, though they did provide, sometimes unwittingly, indirect evidence of persisting male prejudices, e.g. the stereotyping of the male being exempt from duties of childcare or household chores like cooking.

Finally, a few of the subjects in this research mentioned some gender barriers to advancement in employment, and it is true that occupational gender segregation affects the Asian Indian working women in as much as sex segregation characterizes the North American labour market generally. To a lesser extent, this is also true of the gender gap in wages. Many of the women interviewed were computer professionals, physicians, research scientists, university employees, and others who had escaped occupational gender segregation. However, the interviewees also included some Indian American women employed in children's preschools, daycare institutions, old-age homes, etc., and their types of roles are traditionally women's occupations and poorly paid. In some of the newer industries in the Silicon Valley, H-1 visa status foreign immigrants have been working on low salaries in software design, computer graphics, animated video production services, and computer aided design (CAD). Some women are thus employed, but other types of services they used to perform cheaply such as data entry, data processing and business office backroom work, are being outsourced to India and other countries. Regardless, employment in 'technical' positions does not always mean good wages and advancement opportunities for these women.

To sum up, the drive for higher consumption levels and upward social mobility, the pressure of expectations, the ambition to gain status, the possibility of acquiring agency and authority within the family, and other associated motivations have all been influential in pushing the Asian Indian women from out of the home to the workplace. This development leads, as we have seen earlier, to the production of an 'American self' in the workplace, distinct from the 'Indian self' in the Asian Indian home. Therefore, after the analysis of women in the workplace in Chapter II, in the next we turn to the Asian Indian immigrant woman's home and community.

In Chapter III, in attempting to situate the Asian Indian women in relation to their family and the immigrant community, we encounter difficulty in balancing the evidence of the limited improvement in the existential condition of the vast majority of such women despite some small measure of empowerment, with the giant strides towards freedom and responsibility made by a few Asian Indian women with superlatively successful careers. The latter are often held up as exemplary cases, but the less visible majority follow a different trajectory. My interviews mainly revealed that trajectory, though the data on the successful career women is not to be ignored. Among the Indian professional and semi-professional Indian immigrant women I interviewed in the Bay Area, there were a few who had mustered up the courage to reinvent the traditional Indian male-female equation. In such cases, Dasgupta's (1998) claim on behalf of Indian American immigrant women that 'passive or insulated womanhood is not our reality' rings true.

What were the gains even though limited, made by the majority of immigrant women who entered the workplace in the US? One major gain seemed to be access to family resources, ranging from a car and a joint bank account to bigger things such as an education for the advancement of career prospects. The latter is a considerable investment but many instances of this kind of support were found. Moreover, as mentioned earlier, a feeling of empowerment came to the woman once she started to contribute to the family income. It has been reported (Standing 1985) that in India, the woman who works for wages continues to be within the system of gender subordination in the family, due to their wages being low and their lack of control over the uses to which their income is put. It must however be noted that the research also reports that the self-perception of the wage earning woman is still greater than their non-earning counterparts. Standing's thesis may be true of segments in India, but so far as Indian immigrant families in the US are concerned, empowerment within the family is positively associated with the wife's earning status in the family. Standing is of the opinion that access to family resources is one of the prime indicators of status within the family. While comparison over time is difficult, i.e. comparison of the time when the wife was unemployed with the time when she was employed, within the immigrant families interviewed for this study, such access to status was greater for earning wives compared to non-earning wives. Along with this one may also notice a degree of flexibility in the attitude of the husband regarding childcare and housework as the husband is more willing to share such work. Finally, the ability of the working wife to spend money as she likes seems to matter a great deal, as to them, it is a blessing to be part of the American society characterized by high autonomy and high levels of consumption.

What the working women in immigrant Asian Indian families have gained must be considered in the light of the constraints in which she is situated. We first have to consider the fact that a constraint on realizing the full potential of being gainfully employed is that the family demands certain behaviour patterns. The Asian Indian immigrant family contains many stereotypes about the family and male and female roles. This is not unique. It has been demonstrated (Espiritu 1997, 2003) that even though Asian Americans feel empowered by employment in the American labour market, and even though they are glad of the absence in America of interference from the patriarchal extended family, first generation Asian immigrant women are reluctant to attempt to assert equality with their men. They avoid forsaking traditional values and practices for fear of losing their husbands, who are materially, emotionally, and culturally essential for bringing up their children; the family is the seat of their ethnic identity, they do not want to lose it. Likewise among the Asian Indian subjects interviewed in the Bay Area, there is a strong tendency to 'cling' to the family and hence to the marital relationship, although sentiments against patriarchal values of older times may be verbalized. The rationale for clinging to the family is that it is a refuge in times of distress, economic or social, and the bulwark of defence for the individuals who are in a place they do not belong to. For the women, the price to pay for this may be acting out a subservient role to the husband.

There are many small ways in which this happens in everyday life. Almost all the subjects interviewed are in nucleated families in the US, and not in what are called joint families in India. Thus there is space for redefining roles, although the continued reluctance of the husbands to share housework and childcare was clear from what the respondents said and also from their silences. Due to a belief in mothers being the best nurturers for their children, most immigrant mothers, or want-to-be mothers interviewed, rejected the option of fathers performing anything but minimal childcare, although female hired childcare was common among double income Indian immigrant families. Moreover, there was a general tendency on the part of female interviewees to attribute their own success in the workplace to the sagacity or helpful attitude of the husband.

Notwithstanding these constraints, to dismiss the impact of the entry of women into the labour market would still be a mistake. The family in the US is not what it used to be back home in India, nor is the new working woman a replica of the *Bharatiya nari* (ideal Indian woman) inhabiting traditional imagination. The excessively negative portrayal of oppressed and backward women from India, often by well-intentioned feminist radicals, has been criticized by immigrant Indian observers for it negates awareness against these changes (Dasgupta 1998; Mohanty 1991). As we have noted, there is an agenda emerging for the further empowerment of women, for their protection against ill-treatment or beatings at home, and for raising the level of consciousness of rights in immigrant women's organizations such as Maitri and Narika, as well as in the writings of feminist activists and academic critics with immigrant Indian background and knowledge.

With regard to the women's role in relation to the immigrant community, our evidence shows that it is the women who are regarded as the bearers and preservers of culture (Chatterjee 1993). Not only are they expected to enculturate their children in the home but also in the community so that the next generation retains Indian culture, or some imagined version thereof. For example, in the cultural events, religious festivals, national day celebrations, and similar community gatherings, the men usually wear Western business clothes, or shirtsleeves, while the women dress up in traditional Indian saris and salwar-kameez sets. The vast majority of participants in public demonstrations of ethnic affiliations through cultural activities are women for there appears to be a readiness to accept this role. This is perhaps partly because it accords well with the self-affirming emphasis on ethnicity that their own workplace experience demands, a point that was made earlier. One insight suggests that the family is a less important site for identity assertion than the community. Families are relatively 'free to exhibit wide variations and highly idiosyncratic patterns of interaction and adjustment', happily living in the boundaries between different identity concepts. The community however, is more concerned with defining what it is to be an immigrant and the ideational aspects of this experience (Bacon 1996).

The cultural representations of Indianness in community forums are essentialized versions untrue to authentic lived culture, according to some scholars such as Sucheta Mazumdar who is of Indian immigrant background. It has been suggested that the leaders of the Asian Indian community have vested interest in preserving and promoting Indian heritage, in that essentialized constructions of homeland cultural identity help preserve patriarchal authority and discipline rebellious American-born teenagers (1996). Moreover, these researchers contend that the political dividends of being perceived by the Establishment as a 'model minority' are appreciated by these leaders, thus the women of the community are assigned the role of being the standard bearers of the Indian heritage to unite the community. Both in respect of family and the immigrant community, the discourse of Indian heritage is of importance despite being open to diverse readings in the same way that women's status is. It is heartening to note the remarks of an Indian American feminist scholar and activist such as Shamita Das Dasgupta that we should evoke the *virangana* (female warrior) tradition of Indian culture, rather than the cult of feminine dependence on men (1998).

In Chapter IV the construction of the self by Asian Indian immigrant women, mainly professional and semi-professional, in the San Francisco Bay Area is revisited in an attempt to integrate into the theoretical discussion the empirical data and analysis of the preceding three chapters. The analytical concepts of self and identity formulated by symbolic interactionists have been used to examine the degree of Indianness versus Americanness of professional immigrant Indian women in the San Francisco Bay Area. The main area in focus was the interplay between their Indian self/identity and their American self/identity, both of which are of course influenced by an interaction between an inner core psyche and the surrounding social milieu. I have differentiated between Indian expatriate women in the Bay Area on the basis of variables such as the length of residence in the US and the duration of employment in the American workplace. While the focus was on working women in the Indian community, I also studied a small group of non-working women for the sake of comparison.

I divided professional Indian working women in the Bay Area into three categories: (a) recent entrants, that is, women with short work experience of one to two years in the US; (b) medium duration working women with residence and work experience of two to ten years in the US; and (c) long duration working women with residence and work experience of more than ten years in the US. The self and identity in these three categories was compared with that of Indian non-working women resident in the US.

Asian Indians in the US have the urge to develop a positive and diasporic identity that serves their attempts to construct a place in American society. Their perception of social disadvantage in their placement as Brown people or as a racial and ethnic minority, their experience of being looked upon as 'others' by the mainstream population, as well as their acceptance of the fact that they will remain a minority distinguished as 'different' are all part of this diasporic identity formation. Thus, it is possible to read the emphasis on diasporic identity as a stratagem of self-presentation on the part of Asian Indians who reactivate their Indian ethnicity to bolster their self and identity. This reactivation is not perceived to contradict their desire for acceptance in the new country as Americans and their strenuous effort to behave as Americans in the workplace, on the contrary it is seen as a means of securing acceptance. It is the quality of the character of the host society and the tolerance of differences, which allows the strategy to work.

The reactivation of ethnicity happens in a variety of ways in both the private and the public sphere. Ethnicity is displayed to the public in community events, in religious congregations, in public performances enacting Indian culture, in the presentation of a narrative of Indian heritage in prose, and in spiritual discourses purportedly on India's moral superiority. In the Asian Indian home ethnicity is reasserted through the cuisine, the decor, the display of cultural artefacts, in the patronizing of numerous retail shops selling imported consumption items from India, in viewing cinematic and musical productions, and in training children in Indian performing arts. As we have described earlier, Asian Indian women, both working and non-working, play an important role in these processes, especially at home but also in public events.

Emphasis on diasporic identity and ethnicity is essentially a strategy for immigrants who realize that true assimilation is not possible, and that in the perceptions of the mainstream, they will continue to be 'different' and one of the 'others'. This realization only comes after long residence and work experience in the US, hence this reactivation of ethnicity is observed not so much among newcomers, but chiefly in the long duration group described in Chapter IV. Those who have spent many years of their lives on the road to Americanization finally reach a point where they also begin to learn to be Indian once more.

Glossary

aarti	: Worship with lights.
American Born Confused Desi (ABCD)	: A term used to distinguish Indian Americans born and raised in the US from those Indian Americans who were born and brought up in India and immigrated as adults—'ABCD' is part of the immigrant Indian's lingo.
annaprasanam	: A ceremony to celebrate the first solid food taken by an infant (typically at 6–8 months for males and 7–9 months for female infants).
babu	: Sir/gentleman.
bhadrolok	: Gentleman (Bengali).
Bharatiya nari	: Ideal Indian woman.
Bharatiya parampara	: Indian heritage.
Bharatnatyam	: Traditional dance form of Tamil Nadu, origin attributed to Sanskritic cultural authority, Sage Bharata.
darshan	: Viewing/seeing.
deshe	: In the homeland—in this case: India (Bengali).
Desi	: A term used by immigrants from the Indian subcontinent to refer to themselves; it is inclusive of all diaspora from the Indian subcontinent, whatever their gender, religion, caste, age, or class might be.
diya	: Lamp
Griha pravesh	: Hindu ceremony in which a new house is blessed through a special ritual.
haat	: Street bazaar/marketplace.
idli	: Rice cake.

kadhai	:	Indian wok.
kumkum	:	Red powder.
kurti	:	Shirt tailored in the traditional Indian style.
mandap	:	Temple dome.
mela	:	Funfair.
misri	:	Sugar crystals.
namkaran	:	Hindu ceremony in which an infant is given a name.
ora bhalo noy	:	They are bad (Bengali).
pravasi	:	Diasporic.
puja	:	Hindu ceremonial offering.
roti	:	Indian bread.
sambhar	:	A vegetable stew made with tamarind and pigeon peas that is very popular in south India.
saransi	:	Tongs (Bengali).
sati	:	The self-immolation of a Hindu wife on her husband's funeral pyre.
slokas	:	A verse form commonly used in classic Sanskrit poetry.
tabla	:	Pair of small hand drums used in Indian music.
tava	:	Griddle.
urz	:	Islamic holy day.
utsav	:	Festival.
virangana	:	Female warrior.

Bibliography

Afshar, Haleh (1985), *Women, Work, and Ideology in the Third World*, London: Tavistock Publications.

Agarwal, Priya (1991), *Passage From India: Post 1965 Indian Immigrants and Their Children: Conflicts, Concerns, and Solutions*, Palos Verdes: Yuvati Publications.

'American Time Use Survey Summary' (2011), In *Economic News Release, Bureau of Labour Statistics, United States Department of Labour*, vol. 6, Available at http://www.bls.gov.

Anderson, Benedict R. (1991), *Imagined Communities: Reflections on the Origin and Spread of Nationalism*, revised edn., London: Verso.

Appadurai, Arjun (2006), *Fear of Small Numbers: An Essay on the Geography of Anger*, Durham: Duke University Press.

——— (2000), 'Dead Certainty: Ethnic Violence in the Era of Globalization', in *Globalization and Identity: Dialectics of Flow and Closure*, ed. Birgit Meyer and Peter Geschiere, Oxford: Blackwell, pp. 305–24.

——— (1996a), 'Cities and Citizenship', *Public Culture*, vol. 8, no. 2, Duke University Press, pp. 187–204.

——— (1996b), *Modernity at Large: Cultural Dimensions of Globalization*, Minneapolis: University of Minnesota Press.

Bacon, Jean (1996), *Life Lines: Community, Family, and Assimilation among Asian Indian Immigrants*, New York and London: Oxford University Press.

Bailey, F.G. (1991), *The Prevalence of Deceit*, Ithaca: Cornell University Press.

Banerji, Rita (2009), *Sex and Power: Defining History, Shaping Societies*, India: Penguin Books.

Barth, Frederich, ed. (1969), *Ethnic Groups and Boundaries: The Social Origin of Cultural Differences*, Boston: Little Brown Press.

Bhabha, Homi (1994), *The Location of Culture*, London: Routledge.

———, ed. (1990), *Nation and Narration*, London: Routledge.

Bhattacharya, Ananya (1992), 'The Habit of Ex-Nomination: Nation, Women, and the Indian Immigrant Bourgeoisie', *Public Culture*, vol. 5, no. 1, Duke University Press, pp. 19–46.

Bhattacharya, Malini, ed. (2004), *Perspectives in Women's Development: Globalization*, New Delhi: Tulika Books.

Blumer, Herbert (1969), *Symbolic Interactionism: Perspective and Method*, Englewood Cliff, New Jersey: Prentice Hall.

Bonacich, Edna and Lucie Cheng, eds. (1984), *Labour Migration under Capitalism: Asian Workers in the US before World War II*, Berkeley: University of California Press.

Brenner, Suzanne (1998), *The Domestication of Desire: Women, Wealth, and Modernity in Java*, Princeton: Princeton University Press.

Brown, Richard Harvey, ed. (2003), *The Politics of Selfhood: Bodies and Identities in Global Capitalism*, Minneapolis: University of Minnesota Press.

Chatterjee, Partha (1989), 'Colonialism, Nationalism, and Colonialized Women: The Contest in India', *American Ethnologist*, vol. 16, no. 4, pp. 622–33.

——— (1993), *The Nation and its Fragments*, Princeton: Princeton University Press.

Coltrane, S. (2000), 'Research on Household Labor: Modelling and Measuring the Social Embeddedness of Routine Family Work', *Journal of Marriage and the Family*, vol. 62, pp. 1208–33.

Cooley, Charles H. (1902) (1922 revised edn.), *Human Nature and the Social Order*, New York: Scribner's Sons, pp. 183–4.

——— (1998), *On Self and Social Organization*, ed. Schubert Hans-Joachim, Chicago: University of Chicago Press, pp. 20–2.

Das, Gurcharan (2002), *India Unbound: From Independence to the Global Information Age*, New Delhi: Penguin Books.

Dasgupta, Shamita Das, ed. (1998), *A Patchwork Shawl: Chronicles of South Asian Women in America*, New Jersey: Rutgers University Press.

Desai, Rashmi (1963), *Indian Immigrants in Britain*, Oxford: Oxford University Press.

Dhaliwal, Amarpal K. (1995), 'Gender at Work: The Renegotiation of Middle Class Womanhood in South Asian Owned Businesses', in *Reviewing Asian America: Locating Diversity*, ed. Wendy Ng, Soo-Young Chin, James S. Moy, and Garry Y. Okhihiro, Pullman, Washington: Washington State University Press, pp. 75–85.

Divakaruni, Chitra Banerjee (1995), *Arranged Marriage*, New York: Anchor Books.

England, Paula (1992), *Comparable Worth: Theories and Evidence*, New York: Aldine de Gruyter.

Erikson, Erik H. (1963), *Childhood and Society*, New York: W.W. Norton and Co.

——— (1968), *Identity, Youth, and Crisis*, New York: W.W. Norton and Co.

Espiritu, Yen Le (2003), *Home Bound: Filipino American Lives Across Cultures, Communities, and Countries*, Berkeley: University of California Press.

——— (1999), 'Gender and Labour in Asian Indian Families', in *Gender and US Immigration: Contemporary Trends*, ed. Pierrette Hondagneu-Sotelo, Berkeley: University of California Press, pp. 81–100.

——— (1999), 'We Don't Sleep Around Like White Girls Do: Family, Culture, and Gender in Filipina American Lives', in *Gender and US Immigration: Contemporary Trends*, ed. Pierrette Hondagneu-Sotelo, Berkeley: University of California Press, pp. 263–84.

―――― (1997), *Asian American Women and Men: Labour, Laws, and Love*, Thousand Oaks: Sage Publications.

―――― (1992), *Asian American Pan-ethnicity: Bridging Institutions and Identities*, Philadelphia: Temple University Press.

Estrella, Cicero A. and Vanessa Hua (2004), 'Study of Ethnicity and Civic Involvement', *San Francisco Chronicle*, 22 April 2004.

Fisher, Maxine (1980), *The Indians of New York City*, Columbia, Missouri: South Asian Books.

Friedan, Betty (1963), *The Feminine Mystique*, New York: Dell.

Ganguly, Keya (2001), *States of Exception: Everyday Life and Postcolonial Identity*, Minneapolis: University of Minnesota Press.

George, Rosemary Marangoly (1998), 'But that was in Another Country: Girlhood and the Contemporary "Coming to America" Narrative', in *The Girl: Construction of Girlhood in Contemporary Literature*, ed. Ruth Saxton, New York: St. Martin's Press, pp. 135–52.

―――― (1997), 'From Expatriate Aristocrat to Immigrant Nobody: South Asian Racial Strategies in the Southern Californian Context', *Diaspora*, vol. 6, no. 1, pp. 30–61.

―――― (1996), *The Politics of Home: Postcolonial Relocations and Twentieth Century Fiction*, Cambridge: Cambridge University Press.

George, Sheba Mariam (2005), *When Women Come First: Gender and Class in Transnational Migration*, Berkeley and Los Angeles: University of California Press.

Gilroy, Paul (1993), *The Black Atlantic: Modernity and Double Consciousness*, Cambridge, Massachusetts: Harvard University Press.

Gleason, Philip (1992), *Speaking of Diversity: Language Ethnicity in Twentieth Century America*, Baltimore: The John Hopkins University Press.

Goffman, Erving (1983), 'The Interaction Order', *American Sociological Review*, vol. 48, no. 2, pp. 1–17.

―――― (1961), *Encounters*, Indianapolis: Bobb-Merill.

―――― (1959), *The Presentation of the Self in Everyday Life*, New York: Doubleday Anchor.

Gordon, Milton M. (1964), *Assimilation in American Life*, New York: Oxford University Press.

Gupta, Akhil and James Ferguson (1997), 'Discipline and Practice: "The Field" as Site, Method, and Location in Anthropology', in *Anthropological Locations: Boundaries and Grounds of a Field Science*, ed. Akhil Gupta and James Ferguson, Berkeley: University of California Press, pp. 1–46.

Gupta, Sangeeta R., ed. (1999), *Emerging Voices: South Asian American Women Redefine Self, Family, and Community*, Walnut Creek: Altamira Press.

Hall, Stuart (1997), 'Old and New Identities, Old and New Ethnicities', in *Culture, Globalization and the World-System: Contemporary Conditions for the Representation of Identity*, ed. Anthony D. King, Minneapolis: University of Minnesota Press, pp. 41–68.

―――― (1997), 'The Local and the Global: Globalization and Ethnicity', in *Culture, Globalization and the World-System: Contemporary Conditions for the Representation of Identity*, ed. Anthony D. King, Minneapolis: University of Minnesota Press, pp. 19–39.

Hannerz, Ulf (2002), 'Where We Are And Who We Want to Be', in *The Post-national Self: Belonging and Identity: Public Worlds*, vol. 1, ed. Ulf Hedetoft and Mette Hjort, Minneapolis: University of Minnesota Press, pp. 217–32.

Hochschild, Arlie (1989), *The Second Shift*, New York: Avon Books.

Hondagneu-Sotelo, Pierrette, ed. (1999), *Gender and US Immigration: Contemporary Trends*, Berkeley: University of California Press.

———, ed. (1994), *Gendered Transition: Mexican Experiences of Immigration*, Berkeley: University of California Press.

Huntington, Samuel P. (1996), *The Clash of Civilizations and the Remaking of the World Order*, New York: Simon and Schuester.

Jensen, Joan (1988), *Passage from India: Asian Indian Immigrants in North America*, New Haven: Yale University Press.

Kapadia, Karin, ed. (2003), *The Violence of Development: The Politics of Identity, Gender, and Social Inequalities in India*, New Delhi: Kali for Women.

Kearney, Michael (1995), 'The Effects of Transnational Culture, Economy, and Migration on Mixtec Identity on Oxacalifornia', in *The Bubbling Cauldron: Race, Ethnicity, and the Urban Crisis*, ed. Michael Peter Smith and Joe Feagin, Minneapolis: University of Minnesota Press, pp. 226–43.

Kelleher, Elizabeth (2006), 'US Immigrants Fuel Local Economy in Their Home Countries', *International Information Programmes: Global Issues*, Available at usinfo.state.gov.

Khandelwal, Madhulika (2002), *Becoming American, Being Indian: An Immigrant Community in New York City*, Ithaca and London: Cornell University Press.

Kitano, Harry H.L. and Roger Daniels (1988), *Asian Americans: Emerging Minorities*, Englewood Cliffs, New Jersey: Prentice Hall.

Kumar, Amitava (2000), *Passport Photos*, Berkeley and Los Angeles: University of California Press.

Kunzru, Hari (2004), *Transmission*, New York: Penguin Group.

La Brack, Bruce (1988), *The Sikhs of Northern California 1904–1975*, New York, AMS Press.

——— (1982), 'Occupational Specialization among Rural California Sikhs: The Interplay of Culture and Economics', *AmerAsia Journal*, vol. 9, no. 2, pp. 29–56.

Lamphere, Louise, Patricia Zavella, and Felipe Gonzales, with Peter B. Evans (1993), *Sunbelt Working Mothers: Reconciling Family and Factory*, Ithaca: Cornell University Press.

Lebra, Joyce, Joy Paulson, and Jane Everett (1984), *Women and Work in India: Continuity and Change*, New Delhi: Promilla & Co. Publishers.

Leonard, Karen (1997), *The New Americans: The South Asian Americans*, Westport Connecticut: Greenwood Press.

——— (1992), *Making Ethnic Choices: California's Punjabi Mexican Americans*, Philadelphia: Temple University Press.

Leonard-Spark, Phillip J. and Parmatma Saran with the Assistance of Karen Gensbub (1980), 'The Indian Immigrant in America: A Demographic Profile', in *The New*

Ethnics: Asian Indians in the US, ed. Parmatma Saran and Edwin Eames, New York: Prager, pp. 136–62.

Lowe, Lisa (1996), *Immigrant Acts: On Asian American Cultural Politics*, Durham, North Carolina: Duke University Press.

Luhrmann, T.M. (1996), *The Good Parsi: The Fate of a Colonial Elite in a Postcolonial Society*, Cambridge, Massachusetts: Harvard University Press.

Mazumdar, Sucheta (1996), 'Afterword: Identity Politics and the Politics of Identity', in *Contours of the Heart: South Asians Map North America*, ed. Sunaina Maira and Rajini Srikanth, New York: American Writers' Workshop, p. 465.

Mead, George Herbert (1938/1964), *The Philosophy of the Act*, Chicago: University of Chicago Press.

——— (1934/1964), *Mind, Self, and Society*, Chicago: University of Chicago Press.

Misir, Deborah N. (1996), 'The Murder of Navroze Mody: Race, Violence, and the Search for Order', *AmerAsia Journal*, vol. 22, no. 2, pp. 55–76.

Mohanty, C.T. (1991), *Third World Women and the Politics of Feminism*, Bloomington: University of Indiana Press.

Moynihan, D.P. and Nathan Glazer (1963), *Beyond the Melting Pot*, Cambridge, Massachusetts: Harvard University Press.

Ong, Aihwa (2006), *Neoliberal as Exception: Mutation in Citizenship and Sovereignty*, Durham: Duke University Press.

——— (1999), *Flexible Citizenship: The Cultural Logic of Transnationality*, Durham: Duke University Press.

——— (1987), *Spirits of Resistance and Capitalist Discipline: Factory Women in Malaysia*, Albany: State University of New York Press.

Ong, Aihwa, and Donald M. Nonini, eds. (1997), *Ungrounded Empires: The Cultural Politics of Modern Chinese Transnationalism*, New York: Routledge.

Ong, Paul, Edna Bonacich, and Lucie Cheng, eds. (1994), *The New Asian Immigration in Los Angeles and Global Restructuring*, Philadelphia: Temple University Press.

Oppenheimer, Valerie K. (1982), *Work and the Family: A Study in Social Demography*, New York: Academic Press.

Ortiz, Vilma (1994), 'Women of Color: A Demographic Overview', in *Women of Color in the US Society*, ed. Maxine Baca Zinn and Bonnie Thorton Dill, Philadelphia: Temple University Press, pp. 13–108.

Plummer, Ken (1991), *Symbolic Interactionism*, Vermont: E. Edgar Brookfield.

Prashad, Vijay (2000), *The Karma of Brown Folk*, Minneapolis: University of Minnesota Press.

Purkayastha, Bandana (2005), *Negotiating Ethnicity: Second Generation South Asian Americans Traverse a Transnational World*, New Brunswick: Rutgers University Press.

Puwar, Nirmal and Parvati Raghuram, eds. (2003), *South Asian Women in the Diaspora*, Oxford: Berg, imprint of Oxford International Publishers Ltd.

Rajghatta, Chidanand (2001), *The Horse That Flew*, India: Harper Collins.

Ramakrishnan, Karthick and Mark Baldassare (2004), *The Ties that Bind: Changing Demographics and Civic Engagement in California*, San Francisco: Public Policy Institute of California.

Reddy, Narayana V. S., Vijaya Kumar, B. Nalini, eds. (2005), *Women in Development: Challenges and Achievements*, New Delhi: Serials Publications.

Reeves, Terrance, and Claudette Bennett (2002), 'The Asian and Pacific Islander Population in the US', *Current Population Reports*, Washington DC: US Census Bureau, pp. 20–540.

Rosenberg, B.F. and I. Padavic (1994), *Women and Men at Work*, Thousand Oaks: Prince Forge Press.

Roy, Manisha (1998), 'Mothers and Daughters in Indian-American Families: A Failed Communication?', in *A Patchwork Shawl: Chronicles of South Asian Women in America*, ed. Shamita Das Dasgupta, New Jersey: Rutgers University Press.

Safran, William (1991), 'Diasporas in Modern Situations: Myths of Homeland and Return', *Diaspora: A Journal of Transnational Studies*, vol. 1, no. 1, pp. 83–99.

Saran, Parmatma (1985), *The Asian Indian Experience in the US*, Cambridge, Massachusetts: Schenkman.

Saunders, Kriemild, ed. (2004), *Feminist Post-Development Thought: Rethinking Modernity, Post-Colonialism, and Representation*, New Delhi: Zubaan.

Saxenian, AnnaLee with Yasuyuki Motoyama and Xiaohong Quan (2002), *Local and Global Networks of Immigrant Professionals in Silicon Valley*, San Francisco: Public Policy Institute of California.

Sheth, Manju (1997), 'The Immigrants from India: Who are They?', in *Asian Indian Immigrants: Motifs on Ethnicity and Gender*, ed. Brij B. Khare, Dubuque, Iowa: Kendal Hunt Publishing Company.

Shukla, Sandhya (2003), *India Abroad: Diasporic Cultures of Postwar America and England*, Princeton, New Jersey: Princeton University Press.

Sollors, Werner (1989), *The Invention of Ethnicity*, Oxford: Oxford University Press.

Srinivas, Meera (2001), 'My Page', *Indian Currents*, vol. 11, pp. 48–9.

Standing, Hillary (1985), 'Resources, Wages, and Power: The Impact of Women's Employment on the Urban Bengali Household', in *Women, Work, and Ideology in the Third World*, ed. Haleh Afshar, London: Tavistock Publications.

Steele, Claude M. (1988), 'The Psychology of Self-Affirmation: Sustaining the Integrity of the Self', in *Advances in Experimental Social Psychology*, ed. L. Berkowitz, vol. 21, San Diego: Academic Press, pp. 261–302.

Stier, Haya (1991), 'Immigrant Women go to Work: Analysis of Immigrant Wives: Labour Supply for Six Asian Groups', *Social Science Quarterly*, vol. 72, no. 1, pp. 67–82.

Syal, Meera (2000), *Life Isn't All Haa Haa Hee Hee*, London: BlackSwan Publications.

Takaki, Ronald (1989), *Strangers from a Different Shore: A History of Asian Americans*, New York: Penguin Books.

Talwar, Shalini (1984), *Social Profile of Working Women*, Jodhpur: Jain Brothers.

Visweswaran, Kamala (1997), 'Diasporic by Design: Flexible Citizenship and South Asians in US Racial Formations', *Diaspora*, vol. 6, no. 1, pp. 5–29.

Warner, Judith (2005), *Perfect Madness: Motherhood in the Age of Anxiety*, New York: Riverhead Books.

Willford, Andrew (2006), 'The "Already Surmounted" yet "Secretly Familiar": Malaysian Identity as Symptom', *Cultural Anthropology: Journal for the Society of Cultural Anthropology*, vol. 21, no. 1, pp. 31–55.

Williams, M. (1989), 'Ladies on the line: Punjabi cannery workers in central California', in *Making Waves: An Anthology of Writings by and about Asian American Women*, ed. Diane Yen-Mei Wong and Emilya Cachapero, Boston: Beacon, pp. 148–59.

Winant, Howard (2004), *The New Politics of Race: Globalism, Difference, Justice*, Minneapolis: University of Minnesota Press.

Xenos, Peter, Herbert Barringer and Michael J. Levin (1989), *Asian Indians in the US: A 1980 Census Profile*, East-West Centre Occasional Paper Population Series, no. 111, pp. vii–54.

Yanagisako, S. and C. Delaney, eds. (1995), *Naturalizing Power: Essays in Feminist Cultural Analysis*, New York: Routledge.

Index

American assimilationism 137
Americanization, Immigrants and Asian Americans in process of 3–4, 6, 16, 21, 65, 81, 92–3, 100, 106–7, 129–30, 132–3, 139, 147 (*see* code-switching and role-changing)
Appadurai, Arjun 7, 59, 136

Brenner, Suzanne 35, 50

caste 2, 12, 20, 115, 118, 124, 134; discriminations 12; upper 20
childcare 71, 82
code-switching and role-changing 6, 106 (*see* Americanization)
conservatism 53
cultural authenticity 63, 123
culture, Asian American diaspora and 2, 4–8, 10, 12, 17, 20, 36, 48, 55, 58–64, 67–8, 71, 86–9, 91–8, 100–1, 103–5, 107–8, 110–12, 119–21, 123–4, 127, 129–30, 133, 137, 139, 141, 144–6; American 4, 7, 55, 58, 62, 88, 91, 95, 100, 105, 107–8, 110, 129, 141; American global mass 96; ethnic 5, 12, 61, 63, 87, 107, 139; Indian 5–6, 10, 58–60, 62–4, 68, 86–7, 89, 92–4, 107, 110, 120–1, 123–4, 127, 130, 139, 145–6, diasporic 123, nationalist 95; parochial 108; traditional 60; US 101; Western 2, 17, 95–6, 100, 105, 137

diaspora 1, 2, 7, 12, 16, 103, 107, 119–20, 123–4, 137
Divakaruni, Chitra Banerjee; *Arranged Marriage* 77; *Sister of my Heart* 77; *The Mistress of Spices* 77
divorce 40, 64, 82–3, 141 (*see* marriage)

education 25, 36, 70, 85, 124
employment, Asian Indian immigrant women in 2–4, 6–7, 15, 17–18, 23, 28–9, 31–2, 34–9, 45, 47–51, 54–7, 66, 71, 85–6, 93, 96, 100, 108, 113–16, 125–6, 133–4, 137–8, 140, 142–3, 146; paid 3, 32, 38, 55, 57, 86, 93; satisfactory 34
Espiritu, Yen Le 12, 17, 34, 60, 63, 87, 107, 113, 118, 138, 141, 143

feminism 56, 68, 70–2; American 56, 70
fieldwork, enthnographic 29, 31; methodology and perceptions 31
Filipino work-migration pattern 34

Friedan, Betty 81; *The Feminine Mystique* 81

gender 1–4, 12–13, 17–19, 36, 41–4, 52–4, 56–7, 68–9, 71–5, 82, 85, 91–2, 97, 100, 112, 131, 137, 140–3; barriers 42; biases 52; discrimination 42, 44, 52–4, 68
globalization 7, 119–20, 136 (*see* diaspora)
Gordon, Milton; *Assimilation in American Life* 9
Green Card 15, 21–2, 45, 48
Gupta, Sangeeta 17

H-1B visa, immigrant employment and 21–4, 26, 28–9, 35, 41, 45–8, 74
Hart-Cellar Immigration Act of 1965 22
housework, conjugal relationship and 3, 17, 34, 49, 71, 74–5, 82–3, 92, 143–4

identity, multiplicity and change in 1–6, 11, 13, 16, 19–21, 31, 36, 49, 51–2, 54–6, 59, 66–7, 70, 73, 80, 86, 90–2, 94–5, 98, 106, 108–9, 111–12, 115–16, 119–21, 123–4, 127–8, 131–3, 135, 137–40, 144, 145–6; crisis 3; diasporic 2, 6, 11, 13, 59, 120, 123–4, 127, 131, 137, 139, 146; formation 2, 4, 52, 54–5, 70, 90–1, 137, 146; sexual 80
ideology, dominant 52 (*see* women, subjugation of)
illiteracy 51
immigrants, diasporic community and 2–5, 7–18, 21–4, 27–9, 32, 34–8, 40–1, 45, 55–6, 59, 61, 63–8, 70, 72, 74–5, 79–80, 83, 87, 90, 94, 96–8, 100–1, 103, 105, 107–11, 113–22, 124–7, 129–32, 135, 138–42, 146–7; Indian 2–5, 8, 10–16, 18, 23–4, 28–9, 32, 35–7, 40, 45, 55–6, 59, 63–7, 72, 75, 79–80, 83, 87, 90, 94, 96, 100, 105, 107–8, 111, 113–22, 124–7, 129–31, 138, 140; long duration 115, 127, 135; medium duration 94, 146
immigration 6, 8–11, 13–18, 20, 22, 24, 27–8, 34, 46–7, 73–4, 95, 114, 124–5, 130, 132, 136; theories of 13
Indian women in diaspora 60, 89, 139, employed 57, employment of 49, professional 49, 51, 53–4, working 49, 53–4, 57, 92
India Currents 46, 122
Indians, Immigrant Asian 15, 21, 57–9, 63–4, 66, 69, 72, 74–5, 78, 80, 86–7, 89–91, 106, 111, 113, 115, 117–19, 121–2, 125–6, 132, 141–3, 145, 147; racial strategies of 117; women 57, 89, 142
Indian immigrants as community 5, 31, 34, 61, 63, 70, 72, 79, 81, 90, 117, 118, 123, 134
Indianization, acculturation in US and reverse process of 60, 64, 87, 107, 128
Indonesia, perception of career women in 50, 53, 142

job retention and advancement 41 (*see* employment)

language usage 68
Luhrmann, Tanya Marie 12, 112, 123

Malaysia, factory in 51
marriage 14, 17, 37–8, 53, 77–8, 84–5, 89, 133, 147 (*see* housework)
motivation 33, 38, 51, 86, 140–1

Nair, Meera; *Mississippi Masala* 118

Oakland 1, 25, 29–30, 32, 40, 77, 131, 136
Ortiz, Vilma 36

parents and first generation Indian children in US 64

pluralism 9, 11 (*see* Americanization)
purdah 51

racial chauvinism 63
racialization 17, 112–13, 115–16, 119, 137
rape 52
role-changing 106
romance 78, 147

Safran, William; *Diaspora: A Journal of Transnational Studies* 119
San Francisco 1, 3, 6–7, 24–5, 29–32, 40–1, 46–8, 58, 66–7, 69, 71, 76–7, 79, 81, 83, 86–7, 95, 104, 108, 118, 120, 122, 124, 126, 131, 133, 136, 145
San Francisco-Oakland Bay Area 1–4, 6–7, 16, 22, 24–5, 29–34, 40–1, 43–8, 57–9, 62–3, 66–9, 71, 74–9, 81, 83, 85–7, 89, 92, 94–5, 103–5, 108–9, 113, 118, 120–3, 125–6, 129, 131–3, 136–7, 143–6 (*see* Silicon Valley)
sati 51, 124
self, construction of 58, 131, 145; contested 101; diasporic 119; Indian 105; transnational 119 (*see* identity)
self-affirmation 90–1, 93
self-conception 131
self and identity 1–2, 5, 90, 94–5, 127, 131, 133, 137–8, 145–6; concepts of 94, 133, 145; conflicted 56; construction of 1; formation 90
sexual harassment 17, 52–3, 97
sexuality 78, 84, 147; female 84
sexual molestation 52
Silicon Valley, Information Technology industry in 1–2, 21, 26, 29, 32, 40, 44–7, 76, 93, 99, 137, 142 (*see* Bay Area)
Steele, Claude M. 56, 89–91, 128, 140
Syal, Meera; *Life Isn't All Haa Haa Hee Hee* 69

Takaki, Ronald; *Strangers from a Different Shore* 13
transnationalism, motion of 7

United Kingdom (UK) 14–15, 16, 66, 69, 95, 109, 132
United States (US) 2–6, 8–16, 18, 20–4, 26–41, 44–9, 53–5, 57–9, 62–6, 68, 70–83, 86–7, 89–92, 94–8, 100–5, 107–34, 136–41, 143–4, 146–7; Asian Indian women in 55; employment in 3, 28, 34, 45, 108, 134, 138; Indian immigrant women in 37, 70–1; religious frameworks in 65; single women in 33

wage-gap 55
women, American 32, 34, 38, 40, 57, 81–3, 89, 97, 106, 142; Asian 68, 72, 138; Asian American 34, 38
Asian Indian 2–3, 32, 55, 72, 136–42, diasporic 60, 89, 139; immigrant 17–18, 35–8, 42, 44, 56–7, 59, 61, 70–2, 74–5, 80–1, 83–6, 88, 90, 92–3, 101, 107, 130–1, 138–40, 143–5; adjustment problems 17
career for 31, 50, 53–4, 91, 143; economic contributions to family 55, 57; educated employed 57; professional 2, 7, 18, 31, 44, 49–50, 52–4, 74, 95, 112, 137; white-collar 49; young 51, 68; semi-professional 1, 6, 73; middle class 49, 63, 131
working 1, 4, 6, 7, 31, 33, 35, 44, 49–50, 52–8, 69, 71–3, 79–82, 84, 87, 89–90, 92–5, 101, 112, 125, 128–9, 133, 136–7, 140–3, 146; non-working 6, 58, 69, 81, 89, 92, 95, 101, 129, 133, 146
subjugation of, in family 40, 50, empowerment when employed 55, 57, 85; single 33, 37, 140; liberation movement 82

working and non-working women 6, 58, 129–30, 141; comparison 81; degrees of empowerment 81, housework and childcare 82

workplace 2–6, 32, 41, 43–4, 48–9, 52–7, 91–3, 97, 99–100, 105, 107, 128–30, 132–3, 137–8, 140–6; American 2–3, 6, 32, 56–7, 93, 105, 129, 132–3, 140, 146, employment in 133, 146, ethnoscapes of 2, expectations in 6, gender bias in 57, Indian women in 132, self and identity in 55; Indian 41; social interactions in American workplace 39